❤ Happily Ever After ❤

Stacy Chandler

SPECULATORS, INC./TROY, MICHIGAN

Published by
SPECULATORS, INC.
P. O. Box 99038
Troy, Michigan 48099

Copyright © 1993 by Speculators, Inc.

Manufactured in the United States of America

ISBN 0-9639185-0-8
Library of Congress Catalog Card Number: 93-86925

Speculators, Inc.
HAPPILY EVER AFTER

Typesetting lovingly provided by PuPu

Printed on Recycled Paper

Prologue

This book was written for the amusement and enjoyment of lesbians. It does not reflect the views or opinions of the heterosexual population, nor does it necessarily reflect those of the gay population in general.

WARNING! FOR THOSE OF YOU WHO ARE HOMOPHOBIC: PUT THIS BOOK DOWN IMMEDIATELY!!!! THIS BOOK COULD OPEN YOUR MIND OR SEND YOU TO HELL!!! GO DIRECTLY TO YOUR BIBLE.

Dedication

This book is dedicated to the Goddess of my Universe. A woman whom I have had the privilege of loving for more than sixteen years. Affectionately known as "Pook," "Pookie," "Pook Pook," "Pookyness," "Pookness," "Pootie," "PuPu," and "Putums." Thank you, for allowing me to share these life experiences with you.

BILL OF FARE

viii

GLOSSARY

WOMEN: Females of the Homosapien populace. Most noted for their intelligence, adaptability, and fortitude. The preponderant species on Planet Earth.

LESBIANS: Intelligent Women who prefer to love Women.

POOKIE, ET AL.:   My lover.

MY GODDESS: Pook, the Woman who rules my Universe.

CRAPOLA: Accumulated stuff. Abundance of things.

RELATIONSHIP: Period of time two Women spend together as a couple. Anywhere from one week to eighty years.

COUPLE: Two Women who join together with a commitment to love each other.

PARENTS: People related to you through genes or adoption papers, who believe that they can run your life.

RELATIVES: People of distant relation who feel they can run your life.

SOCIETY: A large group of people related by species, who band together in small numbers, trying to convince all of the others that they are right about anything.

EARTH: One minuscule planet in the Universe. Inhabited by Homosapiens, billions of bugs and plants, and a few million animals.

MINUSCULE: Itty bitty. Teency weency. Very, very small. Insignificant.

Meeting Ms. Wonderful

I fell in love at first sight, on September 27, 1977, the instant that I laid eyes on Pootie. We were at a local chapter of a lesbian gab fest. There were fifty other women in the room at the time. I only remembered Pootie. She was the most beautiful woman I had ever seen. I poked the friend that had accompanied me and whispered, "I am going to buy that beautiful woman a briefcase for Christmas." The friend looked puzzled and asked, "WHO?" We had been in this room for only five minutes.

Introductions and a witty life synopsis were expected from everyone. My Goddess spoke, "My name is Pootie." My mind began singing the theme from West Side Story, "*I once met a girl named Pootie,*" instead of Maria. The bulldozer of love had run over my heart and soul and brain.

My introduction came and went. I was brokenhearted having noticed that my Goddess did not swoon over the mere mention of my name. Thoroughly shaken, I went to Plan B.

This group always went to a coffee house after their meetings, so I elbowed my way through the crowd and sat directly in front of her. I was cool...I was calm...unfortunately, my friends and I watched as I turned into a babbling idiot. I stammered and said a lot of stupid things, followed by profuse sweating (I think this is caused by the brain going into fifth gear while your body is stuck in neutral). Everyone ordered coffee. I eat when stressed. I ordered all forty hors d'oeuvres. Later, Pootie said that she had been very impressed with my appetite. Pootie couldn't tell that inside I was waving banners and telling her I loved her, outside I was a smiling, munching, quivering lump. Thank heaven Pootie just happened to be into her quivering lump phase.

Pootie and I have just celebrated our sixteenth anniversary. To preserve our herstory, I have written about our good times and bad in hopes of discovering why we are so lucky.

Opening Lines

One of the most wonderful things about being a lesbian is that ten percent of the female population is gay.

The possibilities of your meeting Ms. Wonderful are endless, from your doctor to your auto mechanic. You will know when you have met her, by an effervescence of spirit that will make you want to dance on clouds. Your heart sings. Your mind says things like "WOW!" and "Whoopie!"

And what sparks this interest? Anything! Her walk, sense of humor, aura, to the rally stripes on her wheelchair. I have known women who have gone back to school, dyed their hair, and lost forty pounds, just because a Ms. Wonderful has entered their lives. There is nothing as motivating as a new love interest. Being in love is the most wonderful feeling on earth.

You say that Cupid's arrow has impaled you, but she hasn't noticed? To make a lasting impression, it is helpful to have a good opening line. A good opening line foists the responsibility of dialogue temporarily, so that you can rack your brains thinking about a witty response, and a great opening line will make Ms. Wonderful notice you.

Good opening lines that I have tried include: "Hi, I love you. Wanna spend the rest of our lives together?" This line is very good because you can tell a lot about a person by the response you receive. Should she respond with: "Sure, but could I finish this (dance/drink/dinner) first?" Know that this woman is adventurous and amiable. This answer shows interest and a sense of humor.

Let's say she responds with: "Are you out of your mind?" All is not lost! This reply could lead to a nice conversation about insanity, which enables you to learn more about her. A good conversation starter.

Another opening line that you may find useful is: "What are your feelings on the new theory of quarks in relation to Quantum physics?" You've got her attention now! The response is usually a glazed stare, and a general dazed effect. This line is only effective if she is not a nuclear physicist. It is helpful to know her occupation prior to using this line; otherwise, her answer could leave you verbally up the creek without a paddle. *"Daaaaaaa"* is never considered witty repartee. This approach is technically called the DAZZLE THEM WITH BULL SHIT THEORY.

The one line that gets a pretty good response is: "If I give you my heart and soul, would you be the Goddess of my Universe?" This could lead to questions about what kind of universe, which enables you to converse on a wide variety of plains, should you wish to.

If the love bug has already bitten you, the odds on you making a fool of yourself with your first meeting are pretty good. It's a hopeful sign if your Ms. Wonderful smiles and doesn't walk away in disgust. Either she likes you or she is mystified by your presence. "Please pass the mustard" worked wonders for me.

Mountains vs. Mole Hills

So, you have found your Ms. Wonderful and the feeling is mutual. How can you determine your chances of keeping this love for the next twenty, thirty, or forty years? Love longevity depends on how many momentous problems stand in your way. Contrary to popular belief, love does not conquer all. The most that you can hope for in any relationship is that a mutual love will help you both weather the rough spots in life. Being able to recognize a mountain from a mole hill is an all important first step.

One of the first issues that you will both have to deal with is PEOPLE POOP. The good news is: EVERYONE HAS A PILE OF PEOPLE POOP. The bad news is: SOME PEOPLE'S PILE OF POOP IS BIGGER THAN OTHERS.

Your pile of poop will include things like prejudices, qualms, emotional problems, politics, addictions and every shitty thing that has ever happened to you that you can't get over.

During courtship, we are in essence measuring each other's pile of poop, and judging whether or not we can adjust. Let us glance at a few piles of poop to see what obstacles may be in the way.

I am a married woman with seven children, but I think I am a lesbian.

If you are a lesbian feminist who has never questioned your sexual orientation, this statement should be K2 poop for you. You do not want, nor have the patience, to raise all of her children until she discovers which way she wants to go. However, if you are a married woman who is exploring your own sexual identity, this will be mole hill poop, because all you want is a few afternoons of unbridled passion per year.

I am worthless. Yes, I have my doctorate in Physics and the Nobel Prize, but I've never really done anything with my life.

If you have purchased a new hair shirt and lash for yourself within the last week, this is a mole hill. Should you be the type of person who is on an emotional high for two consecutive weeks because you have finally mastered the garage door opener...beware!! This is Kilimanjaro poop.

I am an artiste! I see the universe as a palette of color.

This could be mountainous poop if you think that a smiley face is the quintessential symbol of the art world. Warning signs for you should include your love of velvet renditions of anything. This is a no go if you buy a painting to hide a crack on the wall or to match your couch. If a small box of crayons is your color rainbow, stay clear. On the other hand, if you are in a dither because you have been analyzing four hundred paint chips to find just the right shade to enhance the aura in your den, this is a mole hill.

I could never be unfaithful. Monogamy is me.

If you have just returned from your yearly lust fest at the lesbian nudist ranch, where you were again voted the most yielding love Goddess, this is mammoth poop. Conversely, if you have just left the convent and are worried about diseases, this is a mole hill.

I am a vegetarian.

If you are the president of your local cattlewomen's association, or every fall you load up your rifle because you have a yen for venison, this is poop ridge; but if you are looking for someone to supply you with fresh mushrooms to smother it in, this is a mole hill. On the upside you'll be able to enjoy the forest together.

Only you can decide if you want to deal with a mountain of someone else's poop. Knowing your partner's pile, as well as your own, will go a long way in determining the life span of a relationship. Now, all you're both going to need is undying loyalty, boundless compassion, limitless devotion, immeasurable forgiveness, infinite passion, and you've got it made!

To Love And Cherish

Nine months after our first meeting, Pook and I decided to move in together. We were totally unprepared to cohabit. Before one box was packed, we should have sat down and gazed lovingly into each other's eyes and discussed some of the important decisions that had to be made. "Do we want to live in a mansion and eat beans and grits, or something a little smaller so we can have steak once in a while?" "How will we divide expenses and chores?" "Let's share all of our personal eccentricities now, so that we can live happily ever after."

In reality, Pook saw a cute apartment that had to have a deposit NOW. We knew someone with a van. Her lease was up and my rent was due. Rationalizing that "Two can live as cheaply as one," we up and moved.

Ironically, in the thirty-eight weeks, and two million or so hours of phone calls, we never talked about any of the important issues of living together.

Our first problem arose the moment the boxes were opened. Instantaneously, I learned that Poke and I were complete opposites in lifestyles. Pookie is a pack rat. I surmised this while viewing the forty boxes of magazines that she had brought with her. My next clue was the box of her baby toys complete with old bottles and rattles, lovingly wrapped and cataloged. Pook had saved every scrap of paper and every doodad that had ever meant anything to her, and brought it to the small apartment we had rented.

I am a compulsive thrower-outer. No matter what it is, if it hasn't been used in one year's time, out it goes. I donate to all the local charities so that I can feel saintly about giving. Little do they know that I would pay them just to take the stuff away.

I kissed Pook on the cheek and made a mental note that over the next decade, I would change her stockpiling habits.

Neither one of us had any furniture, but being up to our necks in crates, we improvised. Eight crates and a plastic shower curtain became our dining room table. Six crates with a sheet and assorted throw pillows became our couch. Two crates stacked vertically made end tables.

Now, fifteen years later, we have a nice home filled to the brim with real furniture. Oddly, I find myself missing the crates. They were impervious to dents and stains, and they mysteriously offered more storage than we now have with six times the room.

I never changed Pootie's pack rat habits. Our basement is filled with zillions of things that she just can't part with. I learned early on that I will never be able to change PuPu. When you love someone, you have to take them as they are. I just stand back and watch this wonderful woman work the magic that is our lives.

Dividing The Dirty Work

After you decide to live together HAPPILY EVER AFTER, there will be several points that will have to be taken into consideration. One of the first is who will do what chores. Unless you are both independently wealthy and have round-the-clock maid service, you are eventually going to have to share some basic chores. After all, you can only gaze into each other's eyes for so long before someone's stomach starts to growl.

Cooking will probably be one of the first chores you'll do together. Keep it simple. If you have lived on your own for a long period of time, make sure to thoroughly clean out the fridge BEFORE she looks in it. Remember that food should not display mold of any kind, nor should it be able to crawl across the shelf under its own power.

Pook can only cook two different dishes. What once was very cute quickly turned into "If you make spaghetti and popcorn one more time, I'll scream!" I can prepare several dishes. Nothing fancy. Guess who does the cooking at our house?

Both of you will have some chores that you love and hate to do. I hate to do the dishes. My method of soak and chisel does not sit well with Pootie. She does the dishes. Funny, neither one of us wants to see our reflection.

I love to do the laundry. I'm an alchemist when it comes to detergents, boosters, whiteners, and softeners. Unfortunately, the clothes dryer hates me. I keep trying for fresh, warm, and fluffy. It gives me shriveled and mummified. Pootie now sneaks the clothes that she wants to wear more than once to the dry cleaners. She doesn't want to hurt my feelings, so she drops little hints. One morning as I was removing the curtains for their yearly wash, Pootie smiled at me and asked, "Time to shrink the curtains again?" She had a point. What was once billowing drapery could now pass for valances. Brilliant, gleaming, ultra, fresh, white and shimmering, but valances nevertheless.

Luckily, we both agreed on vacuuming and dusting, We hate it. Our dust bunnies are now dust dragons, which we affectionately name. Neither of us leaves the toilet seat up, so no problems there. We have separate tubes of tooth paste, so we can squeeze at our own contort level. We take turns taking out the trash. We have plenty of rags and cleansers to indulge in should one of us get the URGE. Come to think of it, they are covered with dust, too.

You should talk to each other about what you absolutely hate to do. Divide up the chores, keeping in mind that eating and sleeping are not things to get done. If neither of you likes doing dishes, you can buy a dishwasher or plastic utensils and toss them out. If you both hate to do floors, have a cleaning service in when the floor is no longer navigable.

Do not do a particular chore that you hate for years on end; one day you may snap and threaten to kill her with the toilet brush, much to her surprise.

To Have And To Hold

"You never really know a person until you live together." This may be the truest statement of all time. Here are some observations.

FIGHTING

Plan on fighting at least once a month or more. This comes to about twelve or thirteen fights per year. Figure that two fights will be real screamers with door slamming thrown in for effect. Neither of you are going to win them all; you should win about half. A word of caution here: if you are fighting everyday, or one of you are winning all the arguments, better seek professional assistance.

Some days you will come home bummed out, irritable and fit to be tied. Invariably this is the same day that your lover comes home in the exact same frame of mind. This is not the time to bring up her bad habit of running up the charge card. Wait until she is in a better mood.

Pook and I can fight over the stupidest things, from "Why did you leave the potato chips open?" to "Your family never liked me anyway!" And it goes on from there. Profanity is always good. "Your %x@##$*!" "Moi, bunny lips?" is the reply. We can get really worked up and fight about things that happened back in nineteen forty-six. Which is really strange because neither of us was here in nineteen forty-six. There is no right or wrong way to argue. Try not to go for the jugular. If you are angry, try to go somewhere and cool off first.

P.M.S./WORLD WARS FOUR, FIVE, AND SIX

Have you ever had one of those days when life, as you know it, sucks? Your career, the boss, your better half, and the world in general, is just plain shitty? Do not despair. I, too, get these feelings once a month, like clockwork. I feel extremely "meaty." I get overwhelming urges to purchase sides of beef and saddle of lamb. I am not sure what saddle of lamb is, but it sounds very "meaty." These symptoms manifest themselves by my having behemoth bouts of cooking. I will announce: "I've cooked," with my arms raised like a symphony conductor's during a crescendo. "We'll be having a twenty-pound turkey and a fifteen-pound ham, with all the trimmings. Oh, I've whipped up a few pies and cakes, too. The muffins have a few more minutes and then I'm on to the cookies. Six dozen should be enough, what do you think?" It's only six a.m., as Pook starts to eat this queenly feast. I wring my hands and repeatedly ask if it is dry. She is using a spoon; the meat falls off the fork. Somewhere in a past life, I must have been related to cacti, as I am always inordinately worried about the dryness of food--even breadsticks.

I know when Pook's time of the month rears its ugly head. She will be crying over the fact that I did not notice that she washed the car. If she is crying about the car while I am gnawing on a leg of lamb, we hang crosses all over the house and remove all sharp objects.

Marking your calendars ahead of time, for the entire year, does prove rather helpful. At these times, try and be extra considerate. The only advice I can offer is: If you are the one that is sensitive, know that this will soon pass and try not to be a pain in the ass.

Sacred Things

There are sacred things of your lover's that you should NEVER touch. To make matters worse, this unpardonable sin always occurs without your knowledge. You are totally innocent.

You have inadvertently touched, used, or defiled something sacred. You will be able to recognize this event immediately by the look of horror on her face while the sacred object is clutched to her bosom. The conversation always begins like this: "How could you!" You will stupidly reply: "How could I what?"

May I suggest that instead, you throw yourself on the floor and beg for mercy, because the fight of the century is about to begin, and you're gonna lose.

How could you have possibly known that the towel marked HILTON was a cherished heirloom? After all, it was in the bathroom under forty other towels, wasn't it? Do not under any circumstances say: "That old thing!" Even though it is not your fault, you must make amends. Find a new towel at any cost, wash the old one, have the damn thing mounted.

You must NEVER touch it again. Hell hath no fury as a woman's sacred thing scorned.

Phobic Body Parts

It has been my experience that a lot of women suffer from what I call Phobic Body Parts. This body part will be described by the owner as something grotesque. Body Part Phobia can be any part from the head to the toes. There are two distinct components to this phobia: Real and Imagined.

Let's discuss *Imagined Phobic Body Parts.* This reaction will exhibit itself in your first couple of encounters. She will usually point to the said body part and make a derogatory remark about it: "Oh, I have elephant thighs!" You may be looking at this body part while wondering what she is talking about, because the part in question may be exquisite to you. DO NOT laugh this off. She really believes it. This Imagined Phobic Body Part can be dealt with by loving and praising this part above all others. Now is the time to mention that the part of which she speaks is the best part of all. Speak in glowing terms. Remember to always assure her that this is your favorite part. She may or may not ever get over this phobia, but she will love you for disagreeing with her.

Real Phobic Body Parts: Remember, women come in all shapes, colors and sizes. Scars and stretch marks are but a few distinctive characteristics that make us unique. If you cannot love a woman the way she is, then I suggest that you go to your local toy store and purchase a Barbie doll for that truly perfect body. You will notice that the doll has no personality and is unable to love or care for you in any way. Contrary to popular belief, breasts were never meant to be earrings.

Adjusting To One Another

Both of you may have your CRUNCHY times of the day. This is the time of the day, for whatever reason, you are not feeling loving but crabby and hostile. Knowing when you or your lover are CRUNCHY will cut down on the number of heated discussions you will have in your relationship.

I am at my crunchiest when I wake up in the morning. My body and mind resist having to leave the warmth of our bed whether I've had eight or fourteen hours of sleep. I have been this way all of my life. The odds are pretty good that I'll stay this way. Do not tell me any bad news now, or yell about something I did or did not do. I do not become charming, or for that matter, even civil until at least two cups of coffee have entered my system.

As luck would have it, Pookie is at her most loving and happiest in the morning. Pook will often sing, "Good Morning, Sweetie." I snarl in reply. It's a loving snarl, but a snarl all the same. Pook, being the wise woman that she is, will blow me a kiss from across the room and leave me alone for a good half hour. She knows that I love her with all of my heart and soul, but that this is my crunchy time of the day.

Pookie is at her CRUNCHIEST when she comes home from work. For at least one hour after she gets home, she is fit to be tied. She doesn't snarl like I do. She is deadly quiet, with just the tiniest bit of smoke coming from both ears. When we first met, I was foolish enough to think that I could change her CRUNCHY state of mind. Wrong, wrong, wrong! I have been left posing in the doorway stark naked with only a smile, as she has whizzed by without even a "Hello." Now I give her at least an hour to readjust before I utter a word.

If you want your relationship to have a chance of surviving, learn to recognize the crunchy times of the day. Give each other some space and love each other from afar until the CRUNCHIES disappear.

Very Little Assembly Required

You can learn a lot about your lover by having something to assemble together. It doesn't have to be a big project like a DO-IT-YOURSELF three-bedroom house. Try something small, say, a tricycle for a niece. To make this a really fun project, the box must state: VERY LITTLE ASSEMBLY REQUIRED. Make this purchase on Christmas Eve around six p.m. This will insure that you'll both have to participate in having a rotten Christmas.

You will soon notice that women put things together differently. Here are some types to watch out for:

THE STACKER:

She takes all of the parts out of the box and stacks them all into neat piles. This person DOES NOT know how to assemble anything, and is wasting time hoping and praying that you do.

THE EXPERT:

A variation on the previous theme except, she will say things like: "No problem." This will get a tad tiresome when whatever it is has not been assembled in two years' time. However, you will be able to build a new vocabulary from the obscenities uttered.

NON-MECHANICAL:

When asked to pass the allen wrench, she will reply: "Oh, how cute; which one is named ALLEN?" This will always be the same person who talked you into buying something in kit form.

THE BANGER:

A very strange person who firmly believes that one good smack with a hammer will fix everything, including glassware. She is usually connected with the auto industry. Could be an alien life form.

THE ILLUSIONIST:

We all know this person. She has a tool box that makes a BLACK & DECKER catalog look undernourished. She never fixes anything quite right, but she always has the right tool for it.

THE SAINT:

She rips the box open and puts WHATEVER together in record time, never uttering a single cuss word. She says fabulous things like: "Why don't you go watch television while I put this together for you." This woman is worth her weight in gold. A real keeper. Bolt the door before she escapes!

I do not suffer from these delusions. I could not put a plug in the wall socket without specific instructions. All of the local merchants love me for this. They know that I will gladly pay double for anything, if they put it together.

Pook thinks that she is mechanically inclined, and tries to prove it to everyone she comes in contact with. You have to give her an A for trying though. Who else would spend four years fixing the front room lamp? Subsequently, we have a radio that only receives AM channels, a VCR that only records every other Friday, and a television set that suffers from spastic fits every time you touch its remote control. Not to worry. Poke assures me that the electronic industry is working very hard to eliminate those build-in flaws.

Meeting The Family

SCENARIO ONE:

You, your lover and her parents are seated in an elegant restaurant, perhaps enjoying an after dinner brandy. Her parents are smiling. Her dad is talking about what a wonderful person your lover is, while mom is planning a party to introduce you to the rest of the family. You are beaming with pride as you give your lover a little squeeze of her hand and a sly wink. This could be reality IF you are a tennis star or a doctor whose income is well over a hundred grand a year. In all likelihood, this situation is going to be tense.

Remember that her mother has been waiting for someone to grill for the last twenty some years. In her mind, NO ONE IS GOOD ENOUGH FOR HER LITTLE SWEETUMS. So if you are not independently wealthy and not male, you may be in for it. Following are some do's and don'ts that may prove helpful.

For Starters:

Do try and have your first meeting with her parents at your house or apartment. It's much better not to let the maitre d' know all of your business. Being on your own territory has great psychological advantages in times of stress (easy access to toilet, etc.).

Make sure the house is very, very, very clean. Mentally her mom will add points for this.

Dress your very best. This means: change the old plaid hunting shirt. You can be yourself AFTER they leave.

DO talk to your lover beforehand. Explain that you will not tolerate insults of any kind from her parents. Insults come in many forms: "Just how long have you been depraved?" to "How long have you had my daughter under your spell?" This is the time to ask them to leave or for you to exit gracefully. This works well if you're at your house as opposed to a restaurant.

When They Arrive:

Do be as polite as possible. Bring up all of your accomplishments, school, job, etc....

DO NOT talk about your new book, *The Lesbian Manifesto*, unless it is on the best seller list.

DO have a sports game on the television, as her dad would much rather have something else to do. Find out beforehand what he drinks and have plenty of it. Leave the bottle in front of the set and let him relax.

DO NOT talk about how all men are the scum of the earth. Her father will not appreciate it, since he is a man through no fault of his own.

If the conversation turns to AIDS, depravity of lifestyle, etc., try to have the facts. Realize that you will not be able to change their preconceived ideas. Present your best side and DON'T raise your voice at any cost. We're going for the middle ground here, not to make them hate you, keeping your dignity, and getting through this evening.

DO have a shot of brandy before they arrive. It will settle your nerves. *Caution:* You are going for a slight calming effect here, not a comatose state.

SCENARIO TWO:

If her parents are Bible thumping Christians, DO NOT have them over for dinner, EVER; life is too short.

Pets

Lovers may come and go, but pets are for the long haul. If your new friend grimaces at the sight of your "Fluffy," this could mean trouble. If she is not a pet owner, make sure to let them get acquainted gradually. Do not let your long-haired Persian sit on your new friend's lap no matter how cute you think it is. Pets take some getting used to, just like people. Good advice, but it didn't work for Pook and me....

When Pook and I moved in together, we both owned very different pets. Pook has a lovely American Short Hair cat named Smokey. Smokey is a wonderful cat except for one small problem: he loves to chew on anything made of plastic. This includes the cords to the television, stereo, clock, and the window shades. For some strange reason, the electric blanket cord becomes particularly tasty during sub-zero weather here in Ohio. A number of remedies have been tried to no avail, including a particularly disgusting odorous spray that was guaranteed to spurn all felines. This spray didn't stop Smokey from chewing, but it did make the room intolerable for us. Now we keep an extra cord for everything. Try telling your boss that you overslept for work again because the cat chewed through the alarm clock cord.

I came to this relationship with a one-hundred-forty pound problem named Hercules. Hercules is a rather strange dog. He has the memory of an elephant and a body to match. His good points are that he is large, slow, smelly, and very protective. Well, to be perfectly honest about it, Herky hates everyone in the whole wide world but me. Mastiffs are just that way. Hercules doesn't want anyone near me and he will go to great lengths to prove his point. This makes life rather difficult, with me being the only referee between this anti-social dog and everyone else on the planet.

To make matters worse, Herky knows that he is intimidating. He actually smiles after giving someone a nice scare. Pook and Hercules only tolerate each other for my sake. There is no love lost between them. Neither one has taken the first bite.

It is amazing what we will do for our pets. Herky realized a long time ago that I cannot make him do anything that he doesn't want to do. During the ten-year course of his lifetime, he has on various occasions not wanted to: go to the vet, go outside, go for a ride, or go where he is supposed to. This invariably happens when I am in a hurry. Hercules is very smart and has a memory that Einstein would have marveled. He knows that after I beg, scream, plead, cuss, and threaten: "No gravy for a month!" that I will bribe him with a treat.

"Why do we put up with all of this?" our non-pet friends often ask. Because our pets become members of the family. Just as we can't put weird Aunt Agnes to sleep, neither can we get rid of our pets, no matter how much trouble they are. They might poop on the living room rug, but they always love us unconditionally, which is more than can be said for our own species.

Chocolate Covered Helicopters

I have always believed that in a relationship, both people should try to keep the zest alive. Sometimes in this endeavor I get a tad overzealous.

This one year, Easter was fast approaching, and for years prior, I had always given Pookie a basket for this holiday. You are never too old for an Easter basket. Each year the theme was different. One year it was jewelry among the eggs, the next year it was sexy undies. Well, this one year I was stumped. As luck would have it, I was walking passed the local confectioner's display window when I caught sight of the most beautiful chocolate fantasy created on earth. There stood a four-foot high, twenty-five pound solid chocolate bunny. Telling myself that I would eat only rice and water for a month, I entered the store and made arrangements to have the monolith delivered.

Poke was delighted with her Easter surprise, but after the photographs were taken, reality started to set in. We gorged ourselves on the ear tips first, only to realize that we had three feet and ten inches of chocolate to go. For the next six months, we had chocolate for breakfast, lunch and dinner. Anyone who came to visit was not allowed to leave unless she took a few hunks with her. We finally got down to the base which we gave to a close friend who was returning to college. She shared it with fifty of her dorm mates. Even today, the sight of a chocolate bar makes my stomach turn. Oh well, live and learn. Not always....

There was a period of time in my life when I was enchanted with helicopters. I knew that they were expensive and dangerous, but the idea of owning one appealed to me. Hoping that Pook would share my dream, I talked helicopters, brought books and pictures home, and tried to get Pook to have at least an open mind about them. In a relationship, it is much better if you both share a love for a major project; otherwise, the nagging will make life miserable.

Much to my surprise, Poke grew to like the dream too. The term "someday" seemed to make her more open to the idea. One day for a nice surprise, I rented a chopper complete with pilot for an hour. It was my fondest wish that Poke would love the panoramic view as well as the ride. How romantic, I thought. After making my grand announcement, Poke and I charted a scenic route. We planned that she should fly over our house before returning to the airport. The copter was only a two-seater; so after lift-off, I raced home so that I could wave to her from the back porch.

At the appointed time, fly by she did. I waved furiously. On the way back to the airport, my thoughts were of celebration. Poke had a great time and now our plans were closer to reality.

As the helicopter landed, I got my first hint of trouble in paradise. The pilot was chuckling and Poke was a horrible shade of green. As she alighted from the craft, she presented me with her full air-sick bag and groaned in agony. I don't know what happened, but every time I ask her about the ride, all she does is groan, roll her eyes and runs to the bathroom. My new hobby is knitting.

Tribadism

I had thought that I knew everything there was to know about being a lesbian. After all, I had been a practicing lesbian for over ten years. That was until one day in grad school, I happened across the word TRIBADISM. The book stated that all lesbians do this. It must be good because according to this text, TRIBADISM is why we become lesbians in the first place. Mentally, I ran through the clinical names of all the fun stuff we'd done, and TRIBADISM was not among them. The book did not go into further details, nor does the dictionary. Go ahead, look it up.

Not having an interesting topic of conversation for dinner that night with Pook, over the entree, looking hopeful, I asked, "Do we do TRIBADISM?" Pook's face turned a bright shade of crimson. With eyes lowered, she softly whispered, "No." "What?" I asked astounded, "How come? Every lesbian does it; it says so here in my book. How can we be lesbians if we don't do it?"

Pook, ever undaunted by my quizzical nature, agreed to teach me about TRIBADISM to see if we liked it. Well, I am here to tell you, it didn't work for us.   We rubbed everything on everything else, including ears to elbows.   If we'd been made out of kindling, Ohio would still be ablaze.   The only result was a lot of sore muscles and uproarious spurts of laughter.   I may have unintentionally killed the mood by repeatedly asking: "Is it TRIBADISM yet?"

Shopping

The two of you may do everything together in perfect harmony for the rest of your lives. Pook and I are looking forward to your canonization. Luckily, we have learned that we must shop at our own pace, and rarely together.

Pook's idea of a good time is going to the local stereo store, to browse and talk shop. To me, this is akin to going to the dentist and having all my teeth extracted. I did try to adjust, but after forty times of Pook asking different salespersons "Do you have the new ZS 548 super digital woofers?" and their reply of "No, but have you heard the new WQA console ding dongs?" I could kill myself!

My idea of a good time revolves around garage sales. Pook doesn't understand that because something is old, dirty, and utterly useless, IS exactly what makes it wonderful to me. If it's ugly and a bargain, I can't live without it. Pook hates garage sales.

Now, we shop separately, and after an exhausting day, we meet back at home to compare our finds. I am sure that this approach has saved our nerves and relationship more than once.

Pook and I grocery shop together, but with separate carts. This way, Pook can spend forty minutes in the frozen food aisle, contemplating the newest nuked non-edible. I zero in on the no-name-brand section where I feel that I can save millions of dollars over the years. This approach has worked well for us. Pook wouldn't be caught dead in the generic section, and I hate shivering around the frozen food zone.

It will be interesting to discover what your lover considers a staple foodstuff for your home. You will see these exact items selected every week. Pook always buys eggs, canned corn, and artichoke hearts in heavy syrup. We use the eggs and corn, but Pook never eats the artichoke hearts. She saves them. For what, I haven't a clue. We now have fourteen cases of canned artichoke hearts in the basement. Artichoke hearts in heavy syrup is a disgusting edible, which I try to pawn off at parties, thinking that a beautiful soup tureen will make them delectable. My apologies to the artichoke growers of America, but artichoke hearts are gelatinous green bullets. I am sure that the heavy syrup is really syrup of ipecac.

I always have to buy a chicken when I go shopping. I feel safe when I have an extra chicken in the fridge; with one chicken, I can feed two hundred people with an hour's notice. I must admit that two hundred people have never unexpectedly descended on my house, but it could happen. Chicken is mega-versatile. One needs a chicken in the freezer, for those last minute emergencies.

As you can see, these purchases do not necessarily make sense. However, staple purchases enhance your life and make you feel secure.

Pook has a love of facial tissue. One Christmas, I had a truck deliver twenty cases of facial tissue in a variety of brands. They buttress the artichoke hearts in the basement. Pook delights in knowing that she can luxuriate in tissue for the next ten years. On the up side, we are the only family with tissue in every room of the house, in both cars, and even in the garage.

Once a year, Pook and I visit a very expensive mall to see how the other half lives. Others being ones with large disposable incomes. This mall has only designer stores with exclusive merchandise, extremely high prices, and snooty salespeople. One brave day, I asked to look at a small satchel that was on display. The salesperson looked annoyed, but reluctantly showed me the bag. The asking price of four hundred dollars was outrageous. When I showed sticker shock, the salesperson implied that I could not possibly afford this bag, as I must have just slithered out of the sewer down the street. I saw red. My mind snapped. I watched in horror as my hand whipped out the credit card. Snapping it down on the counter I said, "I'll take it!" with a tone of having several of these bags at home cluttering up my closet. I was smug, and for an instant, I thought that I was superior. Being temporarily insane, I was mastering the possibilities of bankruptcy. "I just love this bag!" the salesperson sang, whisking up the card. "Oh, how many do you have?" I inquired. A smile and silence followed. At five dollars per hour paid to sales clerks, not too many, I thought. With a "Good day, Madam," I exited the store, chin held high. I screamed in the car. I had been duped into buying a bag that I did not need and could not afford without giving up fresh meat for months to come. I refer to these episodes as stupid shopping. Pook heartily agrees, much to my chagrin. Me and this bag are going to be together for a very long time. In fact, to get my money's worth, everyday for the next twenty years. None of my friends can tell that this is an expensive designer bag. I have to control myself from waving it in people's faces; Pook says that would be uncouth. I schlepp it over my shoulder, hoping that people will notice that I'm a superior being for owning this bag. I know that the designer is probably swilling margueritas in his Mexican villa, laughing his ass off.

You may find that you and your loved one like to frequent certain stores. I have yet to pass an earring display and not stop to browse. I only have two lobes, but five thousand adornments. Pook loves kitchen gadget stores. She can't cook two different meals, but we own a lot of kitchen utensils. If you ever need escargot forks for twelve, please see us first.

Shopping will be something that you will both do with relish or disdain. If you are as gullible as I am, or like to eat regularly, leave the credit cards at home to diminish your chances of stupid shopping.

Vacations

Eventually, when everything is going wonderfully in your life, you or your loved one will utter that fatal phrase: "Let's go on Vacation!" Beware! This event can easily ruin a relationship.

A vacation is supposed to be a fun and relaxing period of time that the two of you can share together. For Poke and I, this was never the case. Over the years we have visited Florida, California, Texas, Colorado, Chicago, New York City, China, and New Zealand. I have learned half a million things; let me share but a few....

You will never have fun or be able to relax on a vacation. This is due to the room rates that most hotels charge. At over $100.00 per night, relaxing goes right out the window. You will be overcome with the urge to see and do everything humanly possible so that you are not wasting time. This attitude immediately kills all the fun you are supposed to have. A vacation becomes a quest for accomplishment, because every moment is costing you money.

During this time period, you will lose all sense of taste. This may be due to the blinding effect on your subconscious from all the flashing neon lights. Why else would you purchase that pink flamingo with the emblazed logo on its belly?

It is very beneficial if you both visit a place that one of you has been before. This will easily save you five thousand dollars in cab or bus fare, while you are trying to find an obscure attraction.

If you are adventurous with exotic culinary experiences, you will want to hang an extra map in the bathroom. This kills two birds with one stone. I don't want to brag, but I know the longitude and latitude of all the Tibetan mountain ranges.

Your Blue Cross card and your American Express won't mean much in downtown Bora Bora, so leave home without them. You will find that it is very hard to be polite, after you are told that what you had for lunch was not the chicken chow mein that you thought you ordered, but Fido braised and skewered. With the right information, you can boldly go forth into the world with confidence. A word of caution: Take the Pepto; after confidence, it's the next best thing.

If you are going overseas, it will be very helpful to learn these basic life-saving phrases in the local language:

1. *"Where is the toilet?"*
2. *"No, thank you. I do not want sea cucumber for lunch today."*
3. *"You're kidding; that's the toilet?"*
4. *"Do you have a McDonald's restaurant?"*
5. *"I hate to bother you, but I think I'm going to die."*
6. *"No, thank you. I do not want flank of water buffalo for dinner."*
7. *"I will give you all of my money if you take me to McDonald's."*
8. *"Please, please, please, take me to a toilet now!"*
9. *"May I lay down and die right here?"*

Killing With Kindness

As I stood over the trash bin in my kitchen this afternoon, prying yet another lifeless root from its pot of pain, I solemnly vowed never to torture another plant so long as I live. I have a black thumb, and I have to face the fact that flora and foliage frown on me. To be quite honest, they probably scream in agony. Thankfully, I do not hear them.

In my defense I must explain that I am not your ordinary plant killer. You see, I kill them with kindness. A subtle difference to be sure. In a limitless variety of ways, I am able to kill my plants. I kill them with too much or too little water, too much or too little sun, and too much or too little fertilizer. I have noticed that the quickest demise takes place when I sing to them. This may be due to halitosis or my screeching voice, which has been known to empty a roomful of people in two seconds flat.

Every season for the past ten years, a variety of plants have languished all over our house. This has caused me great consternation and mega bucks. The local nursery person sighs while informing me that

Ohio is not a suitable climate for my ficas; sunny California would be much better for them. Me too, I retort. Why this climatic preference was not mentioned when I paid forty-two-fifty for this plant, I'll never know.

The oracle of plantdom will then proceed to inform me of a new secret elixir that is sure to make them bloom. I'm in luck; it's only fourteen dollars an ounce! Thoroughly guilt ridden that I am unable to provide the proper environment for my foliage, I purchase two gallons of this odorous liquid on time installments and hurry home, only to kill again.

My friends now bring over their half dead plants, knowing that I will put them out of their misery. They know that the end will be swift.

Last year for some unknown reason, my insidious kindness crept out to the backyard and on to a sickly elm tree. By staking the root system and applying enough fertilizer, I was able to kill it in no time flat. In September, with its last breath of life, it fell over rather majestically. May the Goddess forgive me; I fell trees. Fortunately, all was not lost. We had an abundant supply of free firewood for the winter.

You will be happy to know that my tropical paradise is wash and wear now. Silk flowers are the only way to go when you are cursed with a black thumb.

Coupons

This morning I was congratulating myself on having the creativity to prepare braised bologna and fruit cocktail for breakfast. Pook was delicately gagging while trying to hide her portion in the dead looking fern on the table. It dawned on me that we had been eating bologna in a variety of hidden forms for over two consecutive weeks. Nay, nay, we are not bologna lovers. We are the innocent victims of the coupon age.

Two weeks ago, the local paper was running a special. So, in the interest of saving a few dollars, we bought more bologna than usual. Well, actually seven pounds, to be exact.

Pook and I are living our whole life through coupons. This leads to some very strange shopping habits. Let us follow the journey of a typical coupon in our life. Saturday morning the coupon arrives and along with four million others, sits and waits patiently until Pook sorts, clips and then places all of them in the appropriate envelopes, which are then placed alphabetically into the coupon box. Time spent on this project is between one hour and two weeks, depending on the free time available. The box is then carried to the car, where we scan the map to find a store that is giving thrice the face value, always in another State. We must now allot two additional hours for driving. When we arrive at the store, we are informed that to get the full forty-seven-cent savings, we must purchase the super jumbo econo pack. Overcome with joy, we gladly lug all of this crapola to the car and once again into the house. Now we have to spend an additional thirty dollars for the chiropractic visit. Our house is often mistaken for the local relief center because of all the fifty pound sacks lined up against every wall.

In Ohio, buying with coupons is only half as revered as buying in bulk. Depending on how you look at it, we are blessed or cursed with numerous factory outlet warehouses. What is really strange is that I am beginning to love huge cavernous unheated buildings in which I can wander around for days. This becomes an exciting experience when you start to wager on if the precariously balanced pitted prunes will kill the fat lady in aisle six. Sometimes, out of exhaustion, you will root for the prunes.

Buying in bulk makes me feel powerful. I am secure in the knowledge that if I run out, I have three hundred more pounds where that came from.

Let's see . . . today we have hauled one huge bag of dog food, cat litter, bird seed, dry milk and canned goods. I can give up my health club membership and add a two-hundred-dollar savings to our account.

Pook and I are not quite as compulsive as some of our friends who have two refrigerators and freezers full of food. We won't really be able to get into that until we can buy that backup generator we have our eyes on. Until then, we will have to be satisfied knowing that eventually our friends will have to come begging to us for their oat bran. After all, woman does not live on steaks and chops alone.

Bowel Cleansing

It was Thanksgiving day and seven of my Sisters and I were pigging out with the traditional gluttonous frenzy. Out of the blue, someone mentioned the virtues of different bowel cleansing techniques. With rapt attention, we all listened closely. The look on this woman's face as she spoke was one of total rapture, and four of the others were nodding furiously in agreement.

My mind wandered over all of the different health remedies that I had encountered in the last forty years. First came cod liver oil, which my mother forced on me daily. This obnoxious liquid from hell was peddled all around the world to promote healthy children. Then there was vitamin A and D, which was hidden in the milk supply so that we wouldn't rebel. After that came vitamin C for colds, beta carotene for curing cancer, and calcium to keep us from the amoeba state.

I took mega doses of vitamin E for years, until I found out that virility was not a viable attribute for a lesbian. Now it's oat, wheat, corn and rice bran for digestion. I am looking forward to the day that we can all graze in the backyard, instead of going out to lunch. If you were a real health fanatic, you would take every letter in the alphabet and even coffee enemas to revitalize your liver.

I snapped back to the conversation just in time to be informed that bowel cleansing would keep me from acquiring any illnesses, and if done on a regular basis, I would live forever. Throwing caution to the wind, I helped myself to a huge wedge of pumpkin pie, remembering that life itself is a terminal disease.

Accumulating Atrocities

Pook and I have just successfully overcome one of the hardest conflicts of our relationship: we bought a couch. We have faced disasters and catastrophes with much less consternation, but buying a couch proved to be a most formidable endeavor.

Getting two people to agree on anything in life is difficult. When you throw in a monumental array of styles and fabrics, trust me, you are courting disaster. It would be very helpful if your mate lets you make all of those decisions by yourself. I didn't get one of those. Pook has something to say about everything that enters our home.

You would think that purchasing a couch would be a rather quick and easy task. How very wrong you are. It took us four months and five hundred furniture stores to finally acquire a sofa. This is due in large part to what one wants in a couch. Pook wanted to reflect her personality, display an art form, and express a sense of opulence known only to the super rich. I wanted something comfortable to sit on and balance a bowl of popcorn, preferably covered in stainless steel for durability.

I, being the practical one, carefully measured the front room, and patiently explained to Pook that we had only eighty-two inches of space for a couch. I pointed out that it was very disconcerting for guests to leap over a large piece of furniture when either entering or leaving the house. This meant that the hideous play pit which was big enough to fill a small auditorium could not even be considered. Muttering something under her breath about my not having any taste, we continued our quest.

The average life span of a couch, including the payments, is ten years. So we tried to narrow our focus to only five hundred divine fabrics and twenty different styles. Leather and plastic were quickly eliminated because we agreed that we didn't want to either *INVEST* in a couch or have to peel ourselves off of it.

Couches are no longer simple pieces of furniture that you just sit on and dust every once in a while. They do everything now. You can repose, recline, heat, massage, and sleep on these beauties. The prices vary from expensive to truly expensive. At those prices, you no longer want to put your feet up on them or eat popcorn. Couches cost about the same as your first used car did.

Let me share with you some acquired knowledge in the hope that it may save your relationship and a thousand gallons of gas.

People come in different sizes. I am a good foot taller than Pook. She does not think that her feet should dangle off the floor while sitting, even though I think it's kinda cute (it makes her bunny slippers look like they are dancing). Measure the length carefully so that when one of you is reclining, you can still balance the popcorn and reach for the remote without too much effort. Take into consideration the wrapping of her ice cold tootsicles with a large blanket; this will save you many popcorn sweep-ups when she probes you, looking for a place to warm them up.

A swatch, is a swatch, is a swatch, and not a couch. I personally refer to them as the swatches from hell. Trust me, a panoramic view of that cute little fabric can turn out to be very, very ugly.

Once the couch is delivered, the room it goes into will start to look shabby. You will immediately notice that you need a new rug, and the curtains aren't so hot either. While you're at it, a fresh coat of paint on the ceiling and walls would be a good idea. Maybe some throw pillows....on and on it goes.

Horrors! Pook inquired this morning . . . Wouldn't it be nice to have a chair to go with the new couch? Not matching, but something unique. She wasn't listening to a word I said about how we should sit cross-legged on to floor to improve our posture!

Assorted Pustules

Pook and I have different feelings about what to share and what not to share in a relationship. Pook wants to share everything, while I hold out for leaving a little mystery. Assorted pustules is a very good example of this theory.

Whenever Pook gets a cut, pimple, or rash ANYWHERE on her body, she will immediately thrust the affected part into my face [as if I had microscopic vision] and ask, "What is this?" My expert medical opinion is due on demand. "Prickly Heat!" is my standard answer. With an exasperated gasp, she storms from the room to examine whatever it is more closely. This gives me enough time to gather whatever is left of my composure, unless I have fainted dead away.

Pook, the loving caring person that she is, will proudly display her pustule regardless of whether it is bleeding, throbbing, or expanding. I must admit that when she had a four-inch gaping slash, my prickly heat diagnosis tended not to be believed.

Pook thinks that I am totally uninterested in whatever malady befalls her. This is not true. I react this way because my mind and sight blank out completely when a pustule is presented. I have a weak stomach. I am not a doctor. I think nothing of calling 911 for an ambulance if I get a mosquito bite.

Yesterday morning as I was resurrecting myself with my first pot of coffee, Pook thrust her open mouth into my eyeball. While pulling her upper lip into a weird configuration, she asked, "Whasst issff thiff?" I screamed hysterically and ran from the room in horror. I had her believing that she had an alien creature living in there. Little did she know that it was her morning breath that had caused this reaction in me. I really had her going for a second there!

I have explained to Pook that I would much prefer NOT to share in these little surprises. This is why doctors go to medical school [a place invented to teach people to gaze at disgusting things at close range]. I would like to take this opportunity to say that doctors could never be paid enough to look at some of the everyday "uglies" with which I have been startled. Me thinks that Pook secretly delights in terrorizing me every once in a while.

When I get some unknown eruption, I do not wear it as a badge of honor, ready to brandish it on some unsuspecting person. I hide IT and pretend that IT doesn't exist. In extreme cases, I will talk to IT firmly, explaining that IT is only prickly heat and command it to go away. This approach has never failed me yet.

"To share or not to share, that is the question!"

Cooking

Early this morning, Pook was standing over the stove frying up something for breakfast. Fear washed over me as I poured my first cup of coffee. Glancing toward the burner, I checked to make sure that the flames were not melting the handle of the frying pan, or for that matter, the ceiling tiles. You see, Pook is to cooking as crematoriums are to dead bodies. Pookie applies the same "speed theory" of microwave cooking to our conventional gas stove which, when she is anywhere near it, resembles a blast furnace. On the bright side, we are probably the only kitchen in the Midwest that has eight assorted fire extinguishers on hand.

Pook does not know how to cook. She once asked me for my favorite pork chop recipe. I left simple instructions. Take six chops, throw in pan. Cover with cream of mushroom soup, salt and pepper to taste. Bake at 350° for sixty minutes, eat.

As I was presented with glowing charcoal lumps that evening, I smiled bravely lest I hurt her feelings. Pook informed me that she was late in getting home.

She had turned the oven WAY up, so the chops would cook faster. Ovens reach up to 550°. Staring at the smoldering charred embers on my plate, I figured she chose somewhere between broil and self-cleaning. Having read that charcoal is a good digestive aid, I even opted for seconds after I discovered how to whack off bite-size bricks with a hammer and chisel. This is love. Love is not gagging, chocking or moaning when it's really terrible.

To her credit, I will admit that she can make soup. Best of all, Pook knows where the best restaurants in town are located.

Try as I might, Pook is still able to get to the stove when I'm not looking. Tonight we're having kilned meatloaf. I wonder what Ms. Manners would say about using a sledge hammer and log splitter as dining utensils.

Pootie Maintenance

It has been my experience that in a relationship, sooner or later, you will do some form of Pootie Maintenance. Pootie Maintenance is any personal task that you do for each other. You might rub her feet, wash her back, or curl her hair.

Back in 1977, Pootie saw me painting my toenails. She said, "That looks nice!" I have been doing her toenails every month since she made that observation. Pootie Maintenance is one of the earliest rituals that will present itself in a new relationship. Pootie Maintenance is the same bonding ritual performed by monkeys, only we, being humans, don't have to lick fleas and dandruff off each other, unless you are into really kinky stuff.

Pootie Maintenance is also an excellent way to express affection for each other without taking all of your clothes off and getting hot and sweaty. Once this task is firmly in place, it will become part of the relationship. If for some reason you decide to discontinue this ritual, she will feel that you don't love her anymore.

Pootie Maintenance can be used to restore peace in a turbulent relationship. You may be into day three of the greatest fight ever known to Lesbians worldwide, but if it's time to curl her hair, you will forego your winning point and do her hair. The shouting may continue the moment the last curler is in, but at least you both enjoyed ten minutes of silent seething togetherness.

Let's say that you give your sweetie pedicures. You are really doing a lot more than painting her toenails. You are telling her that those clammy or hot (depending on the season) feeties are nice enough to hold, cream, rub, and paint, because they are part of her. After all, these are the same wonderful feet that bring your sweetie to you, and stand by you through thick and thin.

Pootie Maintenance is really an act of love. It is very important to choose something that you don't mind doing for her. Otherwise, Pootie Maintenance will become a real pain. Especially since you'll be doing it forever.

Pootie and I do a lot of Maintenance for each other. She does back rubs and general morale boosting (Thank you, thank you, thank you!) I do pedicures and general nagging (You're welcome!)

Cash Clashes

Women hold many different views on how to spend their hard-earned money. Some of us spend like no tomorrow, others pinch every penny. Ideally, both of you will have enough income to meet the outgo. In reality, this is rarely the case. Money and how it is spent can easily become a bone of contention in a relationship. A philosophical attitude about money is helpful. This is why there are stupid sayings like, "Money is the root of all evil" and "The best things in life are free." You can count on one thing, you'll never have enough.

There are basically two types of money personalities. Spenders and Hoarders. Know who you are and who your mate is. Following are a few examples of each:

SPENDERS:
"Save for the future? That's what Social Security is for."
"I could be run over by a bus tomorrow."
"Banks? Oh yea, a place to put YOUR money."
"Can I borrow $XXXXXXX?"

"What are you saving it for?"
"Easy come, easy go."
"Sale, smale, let's get it now."
"I know this cute little designer shop ...."
"Let's party!"

HOARDERS:

"You want to go out to dinner again? We just went in '84. I remember, you had the chicken McIngots and the bill came to almost three dollars!"

"You can never have too much insurance. Your insurance agent is your best friend."

"My savings account yields five and three-quarter percent per annum."

"I have the first nickel my father gave me."

"Don't throw that out, it's still good!"

"Stocks, bonds and annuities are the pillars of life."

"My brother-in-law can get it for you wholesale!"

The attitude you have about money will never change, even if you win the lotto. A Hoarder will look for ways to maximize the yield on ten million dollars and a Spender will look for a new red Ferrari. Once you know how you feel about money, it is good to look for someone that shares your views; otherwise, chaos can ensue. It's easy to recognize the money personalities of couples you know. Their habits tell all.

Spenders will always come over to your house for dinner. You will play monopoly with them for ten years. They will ask to borrow money. They are always broke. Hoarders will stay at home. They are always counting their money or drooling over their stock portfolio. These people are good to know when you want the latest stock market quotes at midnight.

One Spender and One Hoarder: The Hoarder will always complain about what the other one just purchased. The Spender is happy because she now has a source.

Pook and I have very different views on how to spend our money. Pook will shop and spend regularly. Her philosophy is "Get it on sale! We're gonna need it someday." I will save for months only to make one big stupid purchase. These major mishaps are always followed by weeks of agonizing over whether or not my purchase was wise. I try to justify the purchase by its usefulness. "That new bulldozer/law tractor was a smart investment," I will announce triumphantly. "Yeah, you just never know when we'll need reliable earth moving equipment," Pook verbally pokes.

We finally decided to approach a budget scientifically. We had to get note books and ledgers and a calculator and lots of red ink. Tracking our expenditures was time consuming and took all the fun out of shopping. Creative financing let our imaginations show that we saved millions by buying generic, yet there was never extra money in the account.

We are now using our new and improved spiritual budget. Our coming anywhere close to paying all of the bills becomes cause for celebration. After all of the bills have been juggled, whatever is left we refer to as disposable income which we manage to get rid of very quickly.

Weed Whacking

Depending on the season, Pook and I are blessed or cursed with three acres of suburban crab grass which has to be mowed on a regular basis. The past two summers here in Ohio have been so humid that we have been able to grow both mushrooms and orchids in the crevices of our lawn furniture. As you can guess, we are cutting the grass more often than usual.

We have two ways of cutting the grass. We can use the very old and rickety tractor (when it's not in the repair shop) or the semi-self-propelled (you push and it goes) lawn mower. This gives us a choice of either five or eight hours of extra work every week. Pook and I used to share this task until Pook got a weed whacker. This weed whacker has mysteriously transformed her personality into RAMBO THE WEED SLAYER. Her weed whacking ensemble makes her a sight to behold. She wears overalls three sizes too big (because they don't make a size four), gargantuan suede gloves, and clear protective goggles. With the weed whacker slung over her shoulder, held like a

Geiger counter looking for gold, Pook hits the yard with a gusto known only to agent orange.

Not a single dandelion will be left standing. Unfortunately, neither is my flower garden. With a gentle sweeping motion, she is able to fell small trees. Intent in her goal of taming the acreage, nothing is safe in her path. When I mention that the colorful protrusions from the stalks are for the enhancement of the area, Pook says, "Looked like weeds to me!"

When I am not riding the tractor around our love jungle, I am able to keep myself quite busy with poison ivy. This sixty-day leprous rash will get you out of cutting the grass and drive you insane. If you should get a good case of poison ivy, know that the next two months of your social life is dead. You are going to sit at home, scratch, watch TV, and gain at least ten pounds before it's over. If you make it past the first week, you will be okay. Your mind will begin to falter when the four thousandth pustule arrives. You will begin to contemplate suicide by scratching yourself to death with a Brillo pad.

You will get no sympathy with poison ivy. Your friends and doctor will only chuckle. People will ask you stupid things like "How did you get poison ivy?" I tell them that I saw this lovely poison ivy bush and just couldn't help throwing myself in! Day six is the worst. All pustules are at peak itch and burn. They are in full bloom, and pulsating all over your body. This is the day that you drink a lot, and pray that a comatose state takes over your mind.

Around day fourteen, you will discover that scratching is much better than sex could ever be. It will be difficult to pull your hand away, as scratching is close to a euphoric experience now. It's suddenly you against the plant world. Even the Wandering Jew over your sink becomes suspect. It's an ivy, isn't it? On the late evening news, when you hear that the amazon jungle is being torn down, you will jump for joy. On the up side, you will be a horrendous shade of flaky pink from hosing yourself with calamine lotion.

After the rash is gone, you will go directly to your local nursery and ask if agent orange is available in twenty-gallon drums. This is understandable. You will have an urgent need to defoliate the entire yard, or national park that gave you this plague from hell. If you are unlucky enough to get poison ivy twice in one season, you will beg your doctor to put you to sleep.

If someone you know gets poison ivy, be very cautious when you go to visit her. Gently push in a case of calamine lotion through the door first. After hearing the shrieks of delight, then and only then, push in the pizza. Wait another five minutes, if the infected person says, "Come in," you're safe.

In the interest of saving you a few bucks, I am including some valuable tips on lawn maintenance:

1. *Everything looks like grass when it's only two inches tall, including all weeds.*
2. *No one gets down on her hands and knees to examine the grass, unless she is on a diet, and foraging for lunch. If this should happen to you, just mention the nutritional advantages of dandelion root.*
3. *Condos and apartments are FABULOUS because they are maintenance-free.*
4. *Learn to recognize poison ivy, poison oak and poison sumac downwind and from a distance of fifty yards.*

Adventures In Dining

Pookie and I like to go out to eat at least twice a month. We scour our fifty percent discount dinner booklet in order to try new restaurants. The trouble is that these restaurants are usually located in out-of-the-way places; but for half off, we'll go exploring for new culinary experiences. What experiences they have turned out to be!

Our last excursion took us to a restaurant called THE BLUE HERRING. It was located off rural route 45, west of rural route 56, then take the second fork in the road leftish, and proceed down five miles of gravel lane with gorges the size of Nebraska.

I have seen a lot of interesting restaurant decor in my time, but the BLUE HERRING took the cake. This eatery was an old converted horse barn. One table was placed in each stall. Hay was strewn about the floor, which was some cowpokes' rendition of ambiance. Charming. An assorted collection of harnesses and horse stuff were hung on the walls to pique our interest. The whips got my attention!

A cowgirl, outfitted in early Texas ranch wear complete with neon blue cowboy boots, informed us that she would rustle up our dinner. Decisions, decisions. Should I live dangerously and order the Cattlemen's Surprise or settle for an ordinary Buffalo Burger? The side of fries were renamed cow chips. Surprise! They looked and tasted just like cow chips. So quaint. The table had the usual condiments of steak sauce, hot sauce and Alka Seltzer.

While Pookie was gnawing on her Get-Along-Little-Doggie ribs, I moseyed over to the bar to see if I could lasso me a double Bourbon to try and kill the aftertaste, as dessert was yet to come. As I tried to lean nonchalantly on the foot rail and avoid gazing at an opulent display of spittoons, I pondered, "Who dreamed up this round-up from Hell? Could restauranteurs be the most tasteless people on earth? Is decor designed to put us in a state of shock so that we won't notice the food?"

Where are the restaurants of yesteryear? Good hot food, clean, motif-less surroundings where the tab did not induce heart failure?

Out of the corner of my eye I noticed that my Prairie Pudding had arrived and it was flambe-ing its little heart out. Pookie was nervously glancing about, fretting over becoming a fire hazard. With no time to tarry, I galloped back to our table.

When the bill arrived, neatly tucked into its own tiny saddlebag, Pookie announced that next week we were going to a new place called the GOLDEN BUZZARD. Yum! It's good to know that in a pinch, an Alka Seltzer tablet makes a wonderful after dinner mint.

Answers To Stupid Questions

Take my word for it, certain stupid questions will repeatedly crop up in your relationship. The only reason that they are stupid is that both of you know the answers, but she'll keep asking them anyway.

Question number one: **"DO YOU LOVE ME?"** This is by far the most often asked question, regardless of how long you two have been together. Whether it has been two months, two years or twenty. Your response choices are crucial. You can nip it in the bud, or keep some mystery and never answer the same way twice. Following are some helpful hints.

"DO YOU LOVE ME?"
ANSWER: Throw yourself on the floor, grab her by the ankle and say in a loud voice, "Darling, you're the only one I live for! How can you even ask?" Clutch your bosom and look heartbroken, then say, "Without you, I'm but an empty vessel with no purpose in life." If this is done in your favorite department store, she will never ask you this again in public. Hopefully, the

floor is carpeted and you're not wearing your favorite jeans at the time.

"DO YOU LOVE ME?"
ANSWER:

"No, I've been hanging around here for eight years because there's nothing better to do."

Watch out, there are a couple of variations to this question that are very tricky.

"DO YOU LOVE ME MORE THAN THE LAST ONE (MARY, SALLY, ETC.)?"

"DO YOU LOVE ME AS MUCH AS YOU DID MARY, SALLY, ETC.?"

DO NOT answer these questions in a flippant manner because you could easily start World War III.

"DO YOU STILL LOVE ME?"

"No, I stopped loving you last Tuesday; why do you ask?"

Question number two: **"AM I FAT?"**

"No, sweetums! I was just thinking how svelte you're looking. I think you're way too thin! Let's get a pizza and talk this over. We'll pick up a cheesecake on the way home, just to keep up your strength." Now is the perfect time to mention that if we lived on the moon we would be 1/6th of the weight we are now. Gravity is working against us and it's really not her fault that she chose the wrong planet.

Question number three: **"AM I GETTING OLD?"**

"Old? Why you're the epitome of youth. You're like a diamond whose brilliance hasn't begun to radiate yet. People are always asking me why such a young beautiful woman as yourself is happy with me."

Question number four: **"AM I STILL SEXY?"**

"Yes!" Rip her clothes off!!!!!

Playing Cupid

I am an incurable romantic with an overzealous need to match up all of my single friends. As far as I can figure, it must be some kind of genetic illness. Whenever I meet someone who is single, my mind automatically rolodexes every other single woman I know, comparing attributes, hoping to make a new match. This habit may be due to a recurring past lifetime as Noah.

I should know better by now. It's always a disaster when I introduce two women whom I am absolutely sure will hit it off. Pookie always tells me to leave well enough be, but do I listen? Hell NO!

The last fiasco went something like this. I invited Sally and Rita to dinner at our house. They were a perfect match, or so I thought. After all, they were about the same age. Both women are in the same line of work, one being a nurse and the other a lab technician. Rita and Sally had the same interests in dancing and hiking. They shared a love of water, each owned their own boat. They even had the same home state. The clincher, astrologically speaking, was that they were both crustaceans. Sounded like a winning combination to me!!!!

Dinner was scheduled for seven p.m. I believed that a good meal and some nice conversation will spark love. I outdid myself that evening with wine and cheese and incense and dim lights. My house resembled a den of sin, with the appropriate music. You see, their eyes were supposed to meet somewhere around dessert (luscious cheesecake), and arm in arm they were to stroll into the sunset, living happily ever after. Wrong!

Sally and Rita hated each other immediately. It makes for a long, long evening when two people over-babble whilst the other two only grunt their responses. Oh, there was chemistry between them alright, mostly nuclear fission in nature.

At 7:35 p.m. as Pookie and I were putting away the dinner dishes, I was getting the usual lecture of "I TOLD YOU SO!" God, I hate when PuPu's right.

Sally and Rita had to rush off. Seems that Rita's mom had only a few minutes to live. Sally said that she felt an overwhelming aneurysm coming on.

"Okay, so Sally and Rita didn't hit it off," I admitted, "but don't you think that Sally and Betty would be absolutely perfect for each other? We could have pizza and a nice salad and...."

Pootie threw the dish towel over my face and stormed from the room screaming "NO!" My first thought was what's wrong with PuPu, my second thought was whether we should serve ice cream for dessert. I guess I'll never learn.

Creative Endeavors

At some point in your relationship, one of you may try a new hobby. Remember that it takes some time to get a hobby right. Even Georgia O'Keefe made some really ugly paintings when she first began. Following are some basic guidelines for enduring a hobby with grace.

Never under any circumstance break out laughing at what your lover has created. Do not even crack a smile. Bite your tongue if you have to, but do not laugh.

When you are first presented with her creative endeavor, always *oooooo* and *aaaahh*. This gives you time to think of something positive to say. For good measure, throw in a "That's marvelous!" or "You're so-o-o talented!" This gives you added time to get over the initial shock. Ask her to explain IT to you. Repeat the words that she uses until you get a good clue of what IT could possibly be. After her explanation, add a few wow's just to encourage her.

Hobbies are smelly and dirty. This is what makes a hobby worthwhile. Find some personal space for your sweetie's new hobby. May I suggest a corner in the basement directly next to an exhaust vent. This kills two birds with one stone. It keeps the house clean and her creative uglies out of sight. You can tell her that this move is imperative, because you do not want to disturb her creative flow and concentration. Unfortunately, you will have to visit the basement from time to time and lavish praise on whatever IT is.

Never under any circumstance ask her: "What is it?" This question will make you look stupid, even if you are absolutely sure no one else on the face of the earth could recognize IT either.

Enthusiastic praise is the key to weathering a hobby. Let's say that your lover takes up the creative expression of karate. During the first two years, she will be busy breaking small wood boards with her first, foot and ear lobes. You must feign astonishment with the same gusto for board number six thousand and forty-two as you did the first. Pick up those broken pieces, they make excellent kindling. Believe it or not, you will be quite happy when she works her way up to cracking large blocks of ice. This is a Wonderful time to have a party.

If she is into creating THINGS, sooner or later, no matter what you do, she will insist that IT be brought into the house and displayed for the world to see. Never, never, say: "Over my dead body!" Take a deep breath, and find a space for IT.

Hobbies are prolific. This is because there are different phases to any creative endeavor, from the Ugly Lump phase to the Gargantuan Neon Monolithic phase. You can limit your exposure by putting all of her creations into one room. Tell her that you are making her a museum or gallery to store her precious treasures. Mention that the new steel door is only to protect her creations from the elements, and to guard against the prying eyes of jealous competing artists. This helps keep the door shut. As a good lover, your job is not done yet. You will have to introduce this creative alcove to all of your friends.

Years of *ooooooos* and *aaaahhs* are expected. If the stuff is really hideous, you may want to call your friends and clue them in before they come over. If an unsuspecting friend does say something tacky about your lover's creations, you can always assassinate her character after she leaves. "What does *[insert name here]* know about art? She still buys velvet painting of ELVIS."

One more thing: never include a piece of her art when having a garage sale. No matter how you explain that you wanted to share her masterpiece with the rest of the world, that twenty-five-cent price tag will not only crush her creative soul, you will be banished to the couch for quite a few nights.

Unwritten Rules

Unwritten rules are the laws that govern every relationship. Not unlike the ten Commandments, these laws, though not chiseled in stone, are known to you both. These rules define what either of you can or cannot do. You may not agree with your partner's rules. They are usually non-negotiable. Unwritten rules are the firmest beliefs held by you and your other. These edicts are different in every relationship. Some of us use the standard rules ("Thou shalt not eat my movie popcorn"). Others improvise to suit their needs ("Thou shalt not have sex with anyone outside this commune"). Some women have only one or two rules, others may have five thousand.

It is very helpful to know your partner's rules, and whether or not they are specific, encompassing or ambiguous.

My Pookie seems to favor specific rules for our relationship. "Thou shalt not drive my car, borrow my clothes, or use my expensive skin cream." "Honor the credit cards." "Thou shalt not covet the redhead next door, nor the blonde down the street, nor any woman you may come in contact with." "Do not touch my hair on hair day."

I like the all-encompassing rules myself. "Thou shalt not do anything that I may not approve of." "Do not enjoy yourself with anyone but me." "You shall continue to love me with gusto, when I am old, wrinkled and grey."

Sometimes, I have trouble with Pook's specific rules. For example: "Honor the credit cards." Can I run up the balance to show just how much I honor them? Is shopping at Neiman Marcus more respectful than, say, Wal-Mart? Shall I pay the bills with more reverence than usual? Isn't crying while writing the checks enough? Do you want me to say more than one Novena when the bills come in?

Then there is the perilous world of ambiguous rules. If you are not extremely careful, ambiguous rules can get you into very serious trouble. That's because we're stupid enough to assume that we know what you really mean.

"THOU SHALT NOT TOUCH MY STUFF!" Sounds clear enough. What stuff? All of your stuff? Always?

Sometimes? How about in an emergency? Please point out to me all of your untouchable stuff.

"NO FLIRTING!" Can I wink? Is a two-minute look-over too long? Can I ever kiss another woman? On the lips? How many seconds exactly? Please define flirting.

"DO NOT TALK ABOUT SEX WHILE MY PARENTS ARE HERE!" Our sex? Aunt Bertha's fantasies? What if your mother wants technical advice again? Shall we wait till Fluffy assumes the gender correct position to tinkle on their brand new rug?

"THOU SHALT NOT GET DRUNK AND MAKE AN ASS OUT OF YOURSELF AT PARTIES!" Is wearing a lamp-shade too much? Is laughing uncontrollably okay? How loud is too loud? Who defines my obnoxious behavior, you or the person whom I'm boring to death? Please explain drinking too much. When my eyes are red? Muttering? Why is it when I am telling a remarkably witty and funny story, you tell me I'm drunk? "No one was in the room at the time!" is not always a valid reason.

This is just a smattering of unwritten rules that you may encounter. To lessen the fighting time in a relationship, it will be to your advantage to discuss the unwritten rules and nail down all the ambiguities. Knowing the unwritten rules will go a long way in lengthening the life span of your relationship.

In Sickness And Health

If your sweetie is ever hospital bound, there are several things you can do to make her absence and your anxiety more bearable.

Whether the illness is an ingrown toenail or life threatening, it is your obligation to speak of this ailment in a positive light at all times. This is not the time to tell her about your distant uncle who died from the exact same thing. Do not mention all of the bad things you have heard about the hospital, doctor, or nursing staff. It is your duty as a good lover to assure her every step of the way. She will love you for it, and this act of strength will make you feel better too.

PRE-VISIT

Before you go to see your beloved in the hospital, you must decide that this visit is going to be pleasant even if it kills you. Stop off at the library or bookstore and get a book about interesting facts. This will give you something to do when you have to wait, or if your sweetie is unable to be conversationally perky. There is nothing worse than two people fretting over an illness everyday for two hours.

My Pootie has been hospitalized on several occasions. Before I go to visit her, I dress up just as if I were going on a date. I make sure that I look good. I mentally beat down all of the fears and worries, and even practice smiling if I have to. I cry, bite my nails and pace the floor at home; you should, too.

THINGS TO BRING

Take her favorite pillow to her. Spray it with her best perfume and put on a fresh pillow case. This is a much overlooked, yet very appreciated gift for anyone in a hospital. It gives the hospital bed a feeling of home. I also bring a teddy bear. Yes, PuPu is pushing forty, but I know that it gives her great comfort and she hides it under the covers if she's embarrassed.

SHOW TIME

Smile when you enter her hospital room, and immediately go up to her and either kiss her on the cheek or touch her hand. Show her that you are glad to see her. She feels alone, isolated, and probably sick. She needs to know that you love her and are not afraid to be near her. You must exude hope, cheerfulness and love. You are her link to the outside world. Ask her about her day. Follow any negative statement she may make with a positive one, even if you don't believe it. Give her only good news. This is not the time to mention what a shitty day you've had at work, or how you want to kill your boss. Be up! Be positive! LIE!

Since hospital visiting hours are arranged around mealtime, this gives you an excellent way to establish togetherness. Help feed her. Open all of the various containers and have her guess what it might be. Make positive statements about the food. Pootie and I would make little side bets on what color the Jello would be on the following visit. She made fourteen dollars this way. I think she had an in with the chef; she was right every time. If your sweetie is not on a regimented diet, sneak in her favorite snack food. Fancy chocolates are very nice, but sometimes you just gotta have a peanut butter cup. Sit next to her on the bed if there's room. Always tell her she looks magnificent. She wants to feel good about herself.

You will notice that after her meal and a ten-minute chat that you are out of things to say. Whip out the book on fascinating facts and read aloud. Leave the book with her, so you can establish a feeling of continuance by reading it tomorrow. If others are waiting to visit, be polite and leave early.

You can cry, bite your nails, and pull your hair out the moment you leave the hospital. As you drive home, you can yell and scream in the car. I never care what a passing motorist might think. Get it out of your system. You will have to go back in a few hours or the next day. Keep making positive statements to yourself as well. Don't let nagging fears zap your strength. Be extra good to yourself. Have that ice cream or candy. This is not the time to wallow in self-pity, worry or fretting. Positive feelings and statements make positive things happen.

If your sweetie is unconscious, always speak to her as if she were awake. Tell her everything is alright and that you love her. Studies have shown that people can hear and remember what is said to them even in a coma. Always be out of ear shot when discussing the pro's and con's of her medical condition. If God forbid, the end is near: she will know way before you and her doctor will.

You should not expect any comfort from your pootie now. You are the comforter. You must be a rock through this entire episode. You can get comfort from your friends or family or an understanding bartender. If you are too emotionally involved and cry a lot, do not go to visit. Call, send her flowers or strip-o-grams; she'll understand. No one wants someone weeping over her when she is sick.

ENCORE

Call your pootie before she goes to sleep. Tell her all of the loving things that you were too embarrassed to say while the nurse was giving her that enema. Reassure her that she is getting better and that you are coming to see her tomorrow. Ask her what she would like from home. If she gets tons of mail like my Pootie, take only the magazines and leave the bills at home. Remind her that the phone is right next to you should she want to call in the night. If you get a panic call in the middle of the night, you must tell her everything will be alright. You can have heart failure after you hang up.

Don't dwell on how much you miss her. She does not need the guilt of being sick or away.

COMING HOME

Make coming home a joyous event! Make the bedroom clean and fresh. Have a small table next to the bed for tissues and any stuff you think she might need. Dress up to go and get her. Bring plenty of bags to schlepp all of the crapola that has accrued during her stay. It is not unusual to make three trips to the car with crapola before you bring her. Flower arrangements are wonderfully expensive gifts that tend to drip. PuPu and I choose the two arrangements that she loves the most and give the rest to patients in other rooms. The nurses will help with this if you are pressed for time. The look of joy you will bring to others with a vase of unexpected flowers is reward enough.

When you get home, do not hover over her. Ask what she wants or needs and provide it. She may say,

"Get out of my face!" after you have spent all afternoon preparing her favorite soup. Do not be offended. She loves your soup! She is tired, ill or cranky. She'll be better soon. Freeze the soup for later. Everyone needs rest when they come home from the hospital. If you have a large bed and she is not in pain, take a nap together. She will feel very reassured by this. Your calming, positive presence will do wonders for her self-esteem. PuPu and I take a shower together when she's up to it. She says it's because she needs someone to steady her in the shower, but we both know it's for togetherness. If a shower is not possible, sponge baths can be wonderful. Tell her how desirable she is, how nice her skin is. If there is a scar, point out all of its wonderful features. NEVER say anything negative about her appearance.

Months after Pookie's back surgery, she asked me one morning if the scar on her back was ugly. What she was really asking was if I still found her attractive and if I still loved her. I looked at her scar and told her that it enhanced her back, and then I kissed it, while pointing out all of the wonderful miracles of modern science. In reality, PuPu's scar is a plain little line that shows that someone had had to surgically invade her body to fix it. I have her believing that it's the most interesting detail on earth. After all, what does it hurt?

HOSPITAL PERSONNEL

Be polite. They have their job to do. Like nearly all of us, they are overworked and underpaid. Your sweetie is not the only one whom they have to look after. If you want a more detailed explanation regarding her care, go to see the hospital administer. If you would like to show your appreciation for good service, send boxes of good chocolate to the nursing staff. They can't eat flowers. Sign a thank-you card with your sweetie's name and room number. Make sure each shift gets one box. Everyone likes to feel appreciated for a job well done.

Gifting

Pootie had her rifle slung over her shoulder, a hand gun complete with holster, and four boxes of bullets cradled in her arms, as she walked out of the house last Saturday morning. I waved good-bye and taunted, "Don't shoot anyone!" With the door slamming behind her, Pootie was off to her first day of hostage rescue class.

Yes, on every anniversary, holiday, birthday, and the one time she'll never forgive you for staying out really late and coming home really drunk, you will have to make a major purchase.

Pootie and I have been together for sixteen years, and I have bought her on average four gifts per year. I have tried on over sixty occasions to be loving, original, and financially restraining. Giving a gift is an art and a science. Over the years, I had run the gambit of lingerie, flowers, utensils, and bric-a-brac. Pootie's thirty-eighth birthday was looming around the corner and I was out of ideas.

I tried the usual inventive mind trick of thumbing through the Yellow Pages, hoping to stumble upon something to die for. Electrolysis and burial plots were quickly eliminated only because Pootie is relatively hairless and still young and vital. I coddled the bowling ball idea for a few days, having to discard it only because she really doesn't like to bowl. I tried to convince myself that a gift certificate to the local tattoo parlor might be just the thing. I was desperate.

A spark of an idea came to life as I was doing the monthly domicile debris removal. As I lifted my night gown from the rifle majestically hanging on the gun rack on the bedroom wall (Doesn't everyone have a rifle rack hanging on their bedroom wall?), it came to me.

Pootie had received this rifle years ago, but never learned how to fire it. We draped an assortment of apparel over it, thinking that if there was ever an intruder, we could always smack him over the head with it. A rifle shooting course was the way to go! Back to the Yellow Pages. There were several schools to choose from. After speaking to an instructor of a school I had selected at random, I was relieved to find out that the teacher was extremely qualified and that the course was relatively cheap. I could consider a birthday cake and card after all. The instructor told me that Pootie would need four boxes of bullets to bring to school, and of course, the rifle. I said, "No problem!" I sent her a check for the course and she sent me a gift certificate.

I had a problem. I didn't know anything about artillery, let alone ammunition. Pootie needed bullets and this rifle needed a certain size, unknown to me. Caliber, I found out later. Undaunted, I grabbed it by what I thought was its neck (barrel), and holding it at arm's length with disdain, marched right into the local K-Mart at high noon. The saleslady was very attentive as I asked for four boxes of bullets. Three managers appeared from nowhere, and after determining that I was not a weirdo, examined the rifle and told me the caliber. It was a twenty-two. One manager jokingly asked if I was going to start a war. I thought he was being flippant, until I noticed that bullets come in one-hundred count boxes. When I mentioned that these bullets were a birthday gift, he hurriedly totalled my bill, for fear that the giftee might be right behind me.

On Pootie's birthday, I lovingly presented her with two boxes. One contained all four hundred bullets and the other, the gift certificate. Pootie looked quite puzzled after she opened the bullets. She looked quite surprised after she saw the certificate. She admitted that she would never have guessed what I had gotten her! To Pootie's credit and numerous odd gifts of the past, she said this course was just the thing she had always wanted.

Pootie really started to get into it after buying a rifle case, protective goggles and noise reducing ear muffs. She looked like a female version of Yosemite Sam when she was completely outfitted.

The course lasted three weeks and Pootie proudly displays her qualification targets which resemble slices of Swiss cheese. The rifle is back on the rack and clothes are draped over it, only now it is loaded and Pootie knows how to fire it very accurately.

Christmas is coming and I'm back to the Yellow Pages. I wonder if Pootie would like Bungee jumping, Parachuting, or Sword Swallowing Made Simple?

When gift-receiving occasions crop up in my life, I try to be a practical woman. I let everyone know exactly what my wishes are. I give the name of the store, its location and even the sale price of the item, to no avail. The people I hang out with like to express their personality through gifts. I've been dusting a lot of individuality over the years. I hate to admit it, but I love cash for any holiday. It doesn't have to be a large amount. Singles are fine. Nice, crisp singles are wonderful. The total sum is not important; it's the feel of the cash. Nice color, goes with everything! But no, everyone thinks that giving cash is undignified. When did money become a thoughtless gift? You had to go to your local bank. You had to withdraw some (or, in my case usually, all) of your left over life blood. You had to stick it in an envelope. You had to part with it and give it to me. That's a whole lotta thought.

Gifting is something the demons of merchandising created to keep our economy working. Let's say your friends buy you an ugly gift which you have to return. This leads to buying more fuel, not to mention the wear and tear on the car and yourself, which keeps the mechanics and doctors going. While at the store, you buy your friends additional useless stuff, which they have to exchange...on and on it goes.

You may receive some beautiful gifts for the two of you to share. These "Couple" gifts might help foster a sense of togetherness. After all, you will think twice before breaking up a really good set of encyclopedia.

Creating Your Second Language

"Ten million, two, and seven, seven, seven!" I have just told Pootie that I love her, she's sexy, and I miss her very, very much. A second language in your relationship may develop out of the need to communicate something to your partner without letting the whole world know what you are saying.

Our second language started the night I wanted to signal Pootie that it was time to leave a party that we had been forced to attend. Not having learned to be subtle, I stood up and announced, "Let's go, this party sucks!" This made the hostess rather hostile toward me.

Pootie gave me a stern lecture in the car on the way home. The highlights of which included my being uncouth and barbaric. I was instructed that in the future I was to be nicer and keep my big mouth shut. I apologized profusely because we had twenty more miles to go.

Pootie and I devised a system of my pulling on my ear when I wanted to signal her that it was time to go. Ten years later, this ear lobe drags on the floor and I toss it majestically, like a boa over my shoulder, as I walk towards the door.

We needed to say things to each other over the phone on various occasions, so we developed a simple numerical system to refer to basic messages. "1"--I love you. "10"--I love you a lot. "10,000,000"--I love you with all of my heart and soul. "2"--I'm horny. "7"--I miss you. "5"--I am sorry. Etc.... This system seemed to work well, except that my co-workers wanted to know why I returned calls to 277-1000 everyday of my work life. I finally told them it was a phone sex line. My apologies to whoever lives at that number.

We integrated other signals. Some work, some don't. Pootie or I will cough if we think that something is too high priced. That worked until the day I nearly died choking on a piece of chewing gum. Pootie thought the refrigerator we were looking at couldn't possibly be that expensive. Since my normal color is not blue and I don't usually roll on the floor of the appliance dealer, it finally dawned on Pootie that it was not sticker shock that I was suffering from.

A slight scratch on the arm says we're stuck in a conversation and we would desperately appreciate a verbal rescue. This has led many people into thinking that we are infested with fleas. We use the standard nudge of the elbow in church, not to awaken each other but to stop the snoring if it gets too loud.

After seven years, we had refined our language to looks and grunts. One grunt and an eyeball roll means "you've got to be kidding!" Two grunts and a growl tells me to "back off," Pootie wants to discontinue this conversation. One good eye opening stare with panting means I have seen something good. This makes Pootie nudge me hard and we're not even in church.

Creating your second language is a nice diversity. By year five of a relationship, you can finish each other's sentences anyway, so a grunt and a poke adds some zest. I can't put down the body language we use when we're horny without giving this book an "X" rating. I'll let your imagination take over.......

Ten million, Pootie!

Funny Monkey Theory

This theory has evolved from an old adage that my mother shared with me.

If there are two monkeys in a cage, one of the monkeys should try to amuse the other, or the bored monkey will look for a new cage.

You and your lover have been living together for a while and you are thinking that she will stay forever just because you are so fabulous. WRONG! If she wanted boring, she could have gotten married and had three point two kids, a station wagon and a comatose man.

It is your duty as a good lover to provide entertainment every once in a while. This doesn't have to cost a lot of money. She should be made to feel that you still love her very much. Here are some good cheap fun things to do.

Balloons. That's right, balloons. Go to the store and buy a few bags. Blow them all up and place them all over the house. When she comes home, tell her that you are celebrating the fact that she came home to you. Sound ridiculous? She could have gone home to someone else's house. Tape balloons all over your body and give her a pin, for extended fun. Total cost: ten dollars, if that.

Take baths together. Cost: next to zero. You can add romance with lit candles or smoldering incense. If you don't have fancy bath oil, dish detergent will make mammoth suds and softens your bodies while you're soaking in it. The point is to show her that you care. If you don't, someone else will. If you were really totally wonderful, you wouldn't need anyone, you would be completely happy by yourself.

Visit a lingerie shop together. They will let you into the dressing room together. Let her try on everything. You try on something. It is amazing how sexy you can feel in a full-length diaphanous gown with feather trim. Buy two pair of sexy panties and go home. The cost is about twenty bucks, even for designer panties.

Every once in a while, be a little crazy. Sure, you cut the grass and fixed both cars because you love her, but did it make her jump for joy?

Out Of Town Guests

You and your lover's life will be going along smoothly, then out of the blue you will get a phone call. It's your lover's old classmate from college. She wants to know if she can drop by for a quick visit. She has two days to kill between jetting off to yet another adventure, and she is dying to catch up on old times. Your pootie informs you that they were blood pals through Chemistry 101, and that they haven't seen each other for over ten years. Just two days, no trouble at all. Like a fool, you say, "Sure, come on over." This is where the trouble starts.

You want to make a good impression. This means that you have to thoroughly clean the entire house. Your Pootie dusts off her stereo and albums and announces that she is done, that the house is clean. You spend the next two weeks cleaning all of the other areas that Pootie thought were just fine. Every surface must be gone over with elbow grease and Spic 'N' Span. This is your mother's white-glove test times two! At least your mom knows you, and will allow a random dust bunny. This is a stranger, and for whatever reason, you want her to think that you live in a surgical amphitheater everyday of your life. You want this friend to know that your Pootie picked the cleanest, most wonderful lover on the face of the earth. You begin to act like a June Cleaver, with a pinch of k.d. lang thrown in for good measure, even if a lace apron and cowboy boots look weird together. You are about to be checked over and you know it. You chastise yourself for not losing that extra ten pounds this year, and make a mental note to change all of the light bulbs to twenty-five watters after you repaint the entire house.

A note comes before her arrival. She's on a special diet, and allergic to cats. You calculate the time needed for germinating fresh sprouts and wonder if you can substitute some of the green mold you found growing under the kitchen sink. You make reservations at the local cat motel Sher Sha La Femme for the cat, and clean the guest room twice to make sure that there is no cat hair to be found.

Problem number two. You both own two-seater cars, and the friend is in-between skiing trips. You happen to be in-between careers and unemployment checks. You now have to rent a van to accommodate all of the equipment that accompanies the sport.

To make matters worse, you have been given direct orders to wear your good robe and pajamas every night, smile even when you don't want to, and under threat of something worse than death, not to make any disgusting noises in the bathroom.

Finally, the day arrives. The friend is picked up and whisked back home. You despise her instantly. She is drop-dead gorgeous, exciting, intelligent, and captivating. She is saving the world while making millions in her spare time. You suddenly realize that on her accomplishment scale of life, you are a fathom below whale droppings.

Then comes the hard part. You will have to listen to all of their old college stories. You are not allowed to add to the conversation; you were not there. You nod a lot. You laugh at all of the old conquest stories that are just memories. I reminded Pootie that she told me that I was the first, to no avail. You agree that the University was too hard on them for blowing up the lab one Saturday night. You wonder how the mingling of chemicals could be so-o-o-o bonding. It was their conspiracy against authority that made it so-o-o-o wonderful, they explain.

You begin to see your Pootie with new eyes. This solid, quiet woman stayed out all night and partied? All the years you've been together, she falls asleep in the chair by eight o'clock. She marched down main street, topless, in a gay parade? My Pootie? She still blushes when I catch her in the shower. I'm here to tell you that there are only so many cute college stories that you can handle before you want to kill yourself.

To create a little diversion, you finally ask, "What would you like to do?" Sure, we can go mountain climbing, play three sets of tennis and go swimming before lunch. We do it everyday. Right about then, I began thinking that a good brisk nap is major exercise, but I don't dare wimp out now. Sightseeing and eight deluxe meals per day are the only other distractions offered.

Yes, we do eat out everyday. Big over-priced meals are our favorite. Pate and caviar for breakfast, shrimp creole in heavy cream for lunch, followed by a five-pound lobster swimming in butter for dinner. Yes, we wine and dine like this all the time.

The whirlwind activities, college stories, and heavy drinking till dawn are interspersed only by one hundred and forty-five choruses of their Alma Mater. The words and tune are different every time. You become very grateful that neither were cheerleaders. SIS, BOOM, BAH, RAH, RAH, RAH!!!!!

Suddenly the two days are done and it is time for THE FRIEND to go. How could two million four hundred eighty-six seconds go by so-o-o-o quickly?

I am sure THE FRIEND wondered why I pushed her out of the car in front of the airport, while going fifty five miles an hour. I waved and lied, "Come back and see us again real soon!" Throwing the car into fifth gear, and leaving only a trail of grey exhaust behind, I cheered "SIS, BOOM, BAH...RAH, RAH, RAH!!!"

Pootie Admirers

Admirers are women who hover over your relationship. They resemble courteous vultures looking for carrion. These women can be ex-lovers or devotees. Devotees are easy to recognize. They have a puppy-dog look in their eyes, and they are always underfoot. Devotees will attentively listen to everything your loved one has to say and sigh awestruck. Devotees keep you on your toes by letting you know that they want to be next in line. Devotees and ex's can be the reason for grey hair in a new relationship, yours. Following are some helpful hints that have worked for me on occasion.

During the first two encounters, I try to be polite toward a devotee. Only an extremely nice person can be polite forever. I do not have to worry about this. Usually at the third meeting, as the devotee is telling me how lucky I am to have Pootie or how magnificent Pootie is, I announce that my M-16 rifle is back from the shop. I describe how my new rifle will kill an elephant from across a football field, followed by a discussion on how murder is a much overrated crime.

If I am in a festive mood, I will announce that I am an extremely jealous person, and that I hope my therapy works so that I don't have that overwhelming urge to kill again. I must admit that this tactic puts a damper on the conversation; however, if the devotee is thoroughly convinced that I am deranged, she will immediately remove herself from the area.

Ex-lovers are easy to recognize by the snarl you will receive when you are introduced. Old ex's will keep their distance and glare at you from across the room. A lot of lesbians seem to establish close ties to all of their ex's. Some stay friends forever.

There isn't too much that you can do about an ex-lover or a devotee. If they are particularly annoying, just getting them to move out of your vicinity is a plus. Talk to your lover to find out how she feels about them. You should not try to discourage your pookie from having any friends that she may want, as long as they do not hurt her or your relationship. Try not to be put into the situation of having to vie for your lover's attention. Either she loves you or she doesn't. If she loves you, no one on the face of this earth will matter more than you.

Recreational Activities

After the first year, as your passions ebb, you will want to do other things together. This will lead you into the realm of RECREATIONAL ACTIVITIES. A realm not to be visited by the weak of spirit or wallet. RECREATIONAL ACTIVITIES are getting out of hand. No matter what new interest you may have, prepare to spend a bundle on the crapola that goes with the agenda. Every activity comes with its own equipment. This is so that you can appear professional, intimidate your opponents and look as dorky as possible. This is what makes RECREATIONAL ACTIVITIES expensive.

You will learn a variety of TECHNO SPEAK to impress all of your friends. Techno Speak is the technical language that accompanies each sport.

Pootie and I have had our share of RECREATIONAL ACTIVITIES, and I have a basement full of crapola to prove it.

We started off camping. Woods and nature and finding our spiritual selves was the goal. We backpacked and foraged. It all started with a Coleman stove which replaced twigs and matches. We now needed fuel and charcoal briquettes. Sleeping under the stars was replaced with a tent. Then came air mattresses and cots to support the sleeping bags. We had discovered the world of camping accessories. Sneakers were soon replaced with hiking boots and rather expensive jungle clothing so that we looked good and had pockets galore. The old fishing pole was replaced with rods and reels, guaranteed to snare a whale, should one float by. The rented canoe became an outboard complete with motor. Camping was becoming too much work. The schlepping of crapola broke us from this sport. We gave it up soon after the chiropractic bills got out of hand and when we needed a shoe horn to close the overloaded van on our last trip. We entertained the idea of buying a cottage, but we knew we would have to buy a tractor trailer to haul all of the stuff we were going to need. Camping lingo learned: "Where the hell are we?" Broke and extremely tired, we switched to outdoor photography.

The little black box camera was quickly replaced with intricate steel containers to which we added a variety of telephoto lenses. Tripods came after that, then motorized thing-a-ma-jigs, a spectrum of film, which beget camera bags, straps, waterproof cylinders and state of the art compasses. Outdoor photographic techno speak: "Where the hell's the bird?" The little woodland creatures didn't appreciate the fact that we were there at the crack of dawn just to capture them for posterity. Cold and exhausted, we turned to an indoor sport: billiards.

Playing pool led us to lessons and money lost betting that we could sink ANYTHING on the table. Pool cues that would have made Minnesota Fats weep with joy. We had to have carrying cases, chalk and talc for stick and hands. The disemboweling of a room, and the major purchase of a pool table. Suddenly we had to have proper lighting and a rack on the wall for more cues and stuff like billiard ball polish. A complementary dart board, just in case. A small wet bar, to add the appropriate mood. Ashtrays and music. We got so good that nobody wanted to come over and play with us. Lingo learned: "Eight ball in one of the six pockets." Bored and lonely, we tried our hand at target shooting.

Of course, we had to have guns and rifles and bullets. We also had to have safety glasses and vests and gun cleaning kits and ear muffs for noise reduction. Then came range fees and, would you believe, gun shoes? Marksmanship lessons, hostage evasion and suburban survival classes. Lingo learned: "What bull's-eye?" Shell shocked and weary, we turned our attention to archery, which was located in the rifle range building. Lucky for us.

We needed bows and arrows and tips which break with regularity. Hand guards and carrying cases. Glasses, shoes, and lessons. Targets, range fees and finger grips. Quivers with designer logos.

I am sure that some sports are designed around what to do with women's breasts. They have bras to hold you up, down, right, left, and suspended athletically in mid-air. I drew the line at surgical removal for increased accuracy; they came as a set, and a set they would stay. I just sling them over my shoulder and kept going. The cutting edge of techno speak includes: "You're kidding, that's the target?!"

Visually strained and broke, we turned to exercise. We had to have lessons, equipment, paraphernalia, outfits, bras, undies, socks and shoes, head bands, wrist bands, weights, rubber bands, batons, stairs and bikes that went nowhere.   Not to mention the vitamins, mineral waters and towels. Lingo used must often: "God, I'm tired!" Muscular but achy, we tried bicycling.

With bicycling, we needed bikes and water bottles and bike wear and custom seats. Straps and baskets and special tires for subdivision touring.   Radios, Walkmans. Sunglasses, bandannas and hats.   Locks and chains and redesigned handle bars. Bike wax and air pumps. We looked good, we were broke and snow began to fall. Lingo used most often: "What the Hell are we doing here?"   Undaunted, we turned to bowling.

As I remember, bowling was lots of fun.   There were gallons of beer and lessons.   There were also lane rental fees, balls, shoes and bags.   Towels, bowling ball wax, and red satin shirts that had BOWLING MAMAS FROM HELL embroidered on them. Rosin bags and wrist guards completed the trousseau. New cuss words were learned. Question most asked: "Where's that keg of beer?"

Spring had sprung and we gave badminton a whirl. With badminton, you're going to need a net, poles, rackets, wrist bands, head bands, and knee pads. Also grass seed, mosquito repellant, beer, shoes, socks, shorts, shirts and SPF suntan lotion. Not to mention, lots of money for chiropractic visits for assorted strains and sprains, and thousands of birdies.

We are now down to walking. Good, clean, cheap fun. Ha! So far, we have spent over two hundred dollars on perambulating apparel. Then there is the hidden cost factor of Band-aids and corn pads. You will need shoes, suits, Walkmans, head bands, wrist weights, and gum. Repetitive techno speak includes: "Step on a crack and break your mother's back" and "Where the hell's the car?!"

Do not be discouraged, for there is always The Thrill of Victory and The Agony of Defeat.

There is always the agony of defeat. No matter what sport you try, there will either be a six-year-old child who does it better with a smirk on his face, or a ninety-year-old lady who whizzes past you while calling you kid. Then there's listening to expert advice from your lover, because she has five more minutes of experience than you do. Her being right! And that glazed competitive killer look in her eyes, as you remind her that this is supposed to be fun, and she replies, "In your dreams!"

On the up side, there will be the Thrill of Victory. The thrill of victory will include your unnamed source for procuring Deep Heat Rub in sixty-gallon drums, naps, and knowing that the next activity is three days away.

You can guess by now just how much I am looking forward to the RECREATIONAL ACTIVITIES yet to come. We haven't tried skiing, baseball, swimming, golf, tennis, volleyball, fencing, judo or curling. It's a good thing that banks refuse loans for sporting equipment. Otherwise, we'd work our way around to parachuting, which requires the purchase of a small airplane, or bungee jumping, where we'll need a tall building, bridge, or hot air balloon.

Pootie, I'm pooped. Forgive me, but I long to be a couch potato. Good news! This activity won't cost us a dime. We already have a couch, t.v. with remote, and enough garden hose to reach that keg of beer in the basement. On your mark...Get set....

Shelf Life

The one thing I am absolutely sure of is, vegetables should not be able to move under their own power. I, being from the throw-away generation, tend to toss the broccoli when it is commandeering the vegetable bin. When broccoli is challenging your authority, it must go. These little horrors in our refrigerator are due to Pook and I having different time tables for perishables.

Pook believes that any foodstuff wrapped in cellophane is as protected as if it were in a stainless steel, air-tight canister. "That's still good!" Pook pronounces as I point out that the brown potato chips are supposed to be yellow. Her reaction is due to the fact that her motherland offers thousand-year-old duck eggs for sale. She firmly believes that nothing is perishable. "The expiration date on the cheese was in April!" I announce in July. "Oh, that's when you have to take it from the store, not how long it's good in the refrigerator!" Pook patiently explains. "Are carrots supposed to have two-foot roots?" I stupidly ask. "Good sign. It means they are still sprouting. They're still good!" Pook refrains. Beating back the spinach, I rush to close the refrigerator door, lest something escape and overtake the house.

Ditto for canned goods. "Do you think we'll ever use this ten-year-old can of artichoke hearts in heavy syrup?" I inquire. "You never know when we will need it for a garnish." Pook firmly answers. Yeah, it will go great with our puce celery, I think to myself.

In some respects, opening plastic containers of yesteryear can be an adventurous undertaking. Suspense grips every cell in your body as you pry off the lid of a real oldie but goodie. A good rule of thumb is to hold the canister next to your ear to see if any strange noises are emanating. This is a science in itself. Festering crackers make a crunching sound all of their own.

Years ago, when my first grey hair was a catastrophic experience and with my verbal despair of impaling myself on any sharp object, certain that my life was over, it was very reassuring to hear Pootie say, "You're still good, can't throw you away!" From that moment, I developed an allegiance to all perishables.

On the days when I bemoan the fact that my anatomy is shifting southward, or that crow's feet have left their mark, I go to the fridge to comfort myself with something sinful. As often as not, a cucumber will leap out and bounce like a super ball around the kitchen. Now, I just pick it up and lovingly put it back into the vegetable bin and reassuringly tell it, "Can't throw you away just yet; you're still good!"

Quality And Value

Over the years I have noticed that there are certain words that automatically come up when you are about to part with your hard earned money. These words by themselves don't mean anything, yet they are always used in connection with the spending of cash. Let's start with the two most frequently used words: Quality and Value.

Things that have Quality and Value are usually expensive. Cheap things never have Quality but sometimes they have Value. Expensive things always have both, and really expensive things have Quality, Value, and Appointments. Appointments are really details, taken to the outer limits.

Have you noticed that when they drag out those really big words, you know that you're being taken to the cleaners?

Following are a few examples of those words and their true meanings:

TIMELESS: The thing should last until the payments run out.

AT NO EXTRA CHARGE: They are robbing me blind.

CLASSIC: Yes, I am quite sure the ancient Greeks loved their digital wrist watches.

EXCLUSIVELY YOURS: Anyone with lots of cash.

PERFORMANCE: If you haven't bought a trick bear, forget it.

INNOVATIVE: We really had to rack our brains to come up with this one.

HAND TOOLED: Underpaid labor.

CODDLED: Handled very carefully; the boss was watching.

VALUE: We've got you now!

QUALITY: If you leave here with a pint of blood left in your veins, you'll be lucky.

FEATURES: You look like a nincompoop.

DELUXE FEATURES: You are a fat nincompoop.

UNRIVALED AMBIANCE: Term used for stuff costing over ten grand.

To make matters worse, we are supposed to be able to see, feel and smell these intangible things. We see elegance, appointments, style, and features all the time. We feel the performance, quality and value. And who amongst us has not enjoyed a whiff or two of timeless luxury when it was offered?

The only reason I am bringing this up is because Pook brings home a new car every ten years or so. This time while I was having sticker dementia, Poke was very quick to point out all the free stuff the dealer had tossed in, for only eighteen thousand dollars. Glancing over the brochure, I noticed all of the aforementioned words. The real coup de grace came under the heading NO EXTRA COST. Listed there were the words "STEERING WHEEL." Personally, I have never thought of the steering wheel as an option. The horn maybe, but never the steering wheel.

Pook, we have to wake up and smell the authenticity. The car was free, it's the words that are costing us a fortune!

Love Talk

Lesbians will very rarely rip your clothes off, throw you to the floor, and make mad passionate love to you, unless you are very, very lucky, or ask very, very nicely.

In a new relationship, a simple "Good morning!" may be enough to get you both in the mood. However, as time goes by, responsibilities and assorted work projects tend to take over your free time. In an affectionate relationship, eventually a love dialogue develops, so that you can let each other know when it might be a good time for some hot and sweaty R & R.

"Let's do it now!" works, but diversity will add spice to your romantic life. "I can pencil you in on Thursday, from 2 to 2:15" is not love talk dialogue.

It has been my experience that women like to hint at having a sexual encounter. Following are some important signs to look for.

There are basically three times a day when you will be naked. When you get dressed in the morning, when you take a shower, and when you get undressed at night. Should one of you get naked at any other time of the day, this indicates that the naked person wants some attention. This holds true, only if you are not residing at a nudist ranch at the time. If you live anywhere in the Northern Hemisphere, and it is January, this means the naked person wants some attention, NOW! If one of you is wearing anything diaphanous and neither of you are diaphanous in nature, big hint here.

"Let's take a nap!" is good. Avoid this approach if either of you are exhausted. Snoring is not endearing prose. Looking puppy dog like, and following her all around the house chanting, "Wanna, wanna?" sometimes works. Groveling does have its up side. If you start your day off with "#$*x&*#x&#!!!!," that "Honey, baby, sweetie" talk at night will fall on deaf ears.

Even though Pootie and I have been together for some time now, our love making is down to three hours per day, six days a week. If you believe this, I've got some wonderful swamp land in Florida I'd like to sell you. We both try to do things that help foster the lust in our relationship. We still send each other love notes. Everything from cards and poems, to a few pubic hairs in an envelope.   You gotta be inventive!

You will never, never, ever, have sex on the day or night that your loved one gets her hair done.   This time period is known as the sacred hair vigil.   For some reason, the hair can be tossed and wind blown, and even slept on by the owner, but not physically mused under threat of death--yours.   If she is pleased with her hairdo, she will be alluring and playful.   Beware--don't touch that hair.   If she hates it, you won't want to be near her anyway, as the obscenities uttered will include references to you.

You say that you're not in the mood and your sweetie is?   Try to spurn gently.   "Get outta my face!!!" does not make us want to pursue you in haste.

I sincerely hope that your sex life is like enjoying a fabulous Chinese meal: two hours later, you're both horny all over again.

Too Much Togetherness

Your lives as individuals should not cease to exist when you are in a relationship. Just because the two of you are living and sleeping together doesn't necessarily mean that you are both joined at the hip for life. Too much togetherness will kill a good relationship.

If the two of you are constantly together, you will get on each other's nerves. One day out of the blue, you will scream, "Do you have to breath THAT way!" She has probably been breathing THAT way all of her natural life. You will suddenly hate her breathing only because she is doing it right next to you. This is a clear sign that you are spending too much time together. There are other signs to look out for. Your sweetie says she may visit her sister for the weekend. You help her pack, gas up the car, and wave goodbye enthusiastically, before she has even made up her mind to go. When someone asks, "What's new?" and neither of you responds. The clincher is when you find yourselves finishing each other's sentences.

If you are still fluffing up her pillows and sharing one toothbrush, I can bet that you are in a new relationship. To the six couples on the face of this earth who have lived, worked and slept together for the last fifty years, I congratulate you. I am talking about all of the rest of us who know better.

Human beings learned a long time ago that we must separate every once in a while so that we don't kill each other. This is why social events, sleep, and jobs were invented. A little time away from each other is a good thing. To help ease the togetherness tension, may I suggest mini partings. Pook and I will often go to a cinema complex and see two different movies at two different theaters. This gives us something new to discuss on the car ride home. Not to mention the added bonus of having the popcorn all to yourself.

To keep a strong lasting relationship, I do not recommend working together. The overly optimistic, who choose or are thrust into working together for better or worse, quickly find out that this lifestyle makes some things better, and some things much worse. Working, succeeding, and being with each other every waking moment will put an added strain on any relationship.

If you are thinking about a joint working venture, there are many things to consider. Do you both get along? You will say, "Of course, we love each other!" One way to find out if that statement is true is to jot down the time and dates of your fights. If the monthly numbers change, you are ahead. If you fight and argue every two to three days, know that this will increase dramatically when you are working together. New elements enter your relationship when you work side by side. Competitiveness, decisions, and management styles rear their ugly heads.

It will be very hard to act professional all day long, and then be warm and loving at night. This problem gets worse, if one of you is in a higher position at the work place. You may find it very difficult to be warm and cuddly after she has been barking orders at you all day. It will not help make for an exciting relationship at home, when the work place conversation continues and you are both eating and sleeping in the business mode. It is impossible to be a boss, competitive, or struggling, and still be a pootie.

Thankfully, Pook and I have two different occupations. We do share a part-time business venture. Our relationship would not survive if we had to work together, everyday. Pook is a perfectionist. Unless she does it, it is never done right. I am result oriented. I want it done now. We have been able to negotiate these two different management styles by finding our own niche. I do the things that have to be done now, and Pook does the things that have to be done perfectly. Through trial and error, we learned how to separate a work relationship from our home relationship.

Whoever said, "Parting is such sweet sorrow" hit the nail right on the head. In the early years of your relationship, a few days away from each other may seem like the end of the world. For those of us who have been in a long-term relationship, a short parting sometimes is a godsend. Pootie parting should not be met with sadness. I do not recommend that you jump for joy in front of her either.

There are lots of things you can do to keep yourself amused while she is gone. You have the house to yourself. You can run around naked, and not be preyed upon. You can scratch wherever it itches. You can stay up as late as you want, and completely control the television set. You can have pizza and beer for breakfast. You can go to the restaurant that your Pootie won't try. You can munch on antacid tablets, after your visit to Chez Burrito Hell, and not have to listen to "I told you so!" You can play music as loud and late as you would like. You cannot have any women over that your Pootie is remotely jealous of. You can't go to the gay bars and stay out all night.

When my Pootie is away, I usually clean the house, run around naked for five minutes (that's as long as I can hold my stomach in), and eat strange food, waiting for Pootie's nightly call. I listen to my old Beatles records, and scratch when something itches. I assure myself that I am the helmswoman of my ship and the mistress of my destiny. It takes about two days to get over these delusions.

I learn that when you control the television set, nothing is ever on. Pizza and beer give you gas. Eating out alone is boring. Sleeping alone is very boring. Actually, the only thing I've ever really learned is that I miss my Pootie a lot.

Your Unthwarted Rival

You may be thinking about all of your lover's ex's, or that gorgeous redhead at her work place. Oh, if it were but that simple. Another woman is an easy task to eliminate from your relationship. I'm talking real, undying love. A passion unequaled by mortal beings. I'm talking your partner's love of a thing. Be it cars, stereos, or computers. Eventually, you will have to come to terms with your unthwarted rival.

Pootie loves stereo equipment. The more knobs, switches and dials, the better. How are ya going to compete with twenty buttons, levers, and meters? I have two, maybe three interesting lumps on my entire body. I cannot glisten nor captivate one millionth as much as her new power amplifier.

Has anyone checked to see if these gadgets electronically induce orgasmic response? When a new piece of stereo equipment arrives, Pootie's eyes are all aglow. She breathes harder, she sweats, her face is flush. She's excited.

It's not just the stereo doodads. I could live with those. It's living the audiophile life that bothers me.

Pootie reads her stereo magazine with more gusto than I view Lesbian Volleyball Nudes. She polishes the speaker veneer with more passion than our foreplay.

Pootie's idea of a good time is to spend a perfectly good Saturday morning and afternoon going to have a look-see. Astronomical pricing makes it impossible to purchase. A true audiophile goes, looks, sees, and listens a lot, before actually bringing a new piece home. Audiophiles pray for inheritances, winning the lottery, and acts of God, so that they can "upgrade." Once inside, she banters with the sales staff for hours in stereo speak, a language known only to electronically brain linked people. I have personally witnessed profound discussions on the eletrical variances of power strips, which have lasted for two hours.

Last Saturday, just for fun, after I had listened to why this new needle (which cost more than all of my albums put together) was the state-of-the-art, I flippantly told the salesperson that a little tape and a nickel worked just fine for me. With everyone all aghast, I was sent out to the car because I had defiled the aura of the audiophile world.

Being an audiophile takes too much time. I like to slap a record on, or throw a tape in, and listen to music now. Pootie has to turn on all of her equipment so that it warms up. She has to condition the needle and adjust the turntable. Then she has to take out an album, vacuum wash it and bathe it in preservatives that cost more than my favorate perfume. She then chants and turns three times to the east before playing whatever music she has chosen. All of these procedures cut down on the foot stomping, thigh slapping time allotted.

All of this equipment is regally stationed on a solid steel tower in our front room. I am forbidden to even look in its direction. I absolutely refuse to genuflect in its presence.

And heaven forbid I should ask for a tape for the car! This is akin to ripping the prodigal from its mother's left teat. I must swear on a stack of Bibles that I will remove this tape from the car the millisecond I hit our driveway. Depending on the tapes programmed vibrations for the day, I must promise to push on or off the DSP button, and the chrome button, and the Dolby button. I now listen to the radio in my car, too timid to enter the audiophile world.

If there is a new stereo store opening anywhere in our area on a Saturday afternoon, my only hope is to pray for a power outage statewide if I want to indulge in something a tad more interesting.

I have come to terms with my unthwarted rival. I am not beneath taping stereo pictures and articles to my body, for a more exciting review.

No doubt about it, stereo equipment rules, and I am but a passing fancy.

Going To The Movies

Pootie and I are avid movie goers. We evolved, so to speak, because going to a play or sporting event was becoming outrageously expensive. In an effort to kid ourselves that we are culturally enriched, we try to intersperse artsy movies with Godzilla '89. This combines mental gymnastics with brain dead amusement. We take a democratic approach to our movie selections. "I'll go see 'The Thing From Mars' with you if you'll see 'The Bostonians' with me." Pook challenges.

On very rare occasions, we see two movies back to back. This leads to many interesting discussions. Our last intellectual discourse went something like this. "Wasn't that rainbow over the Netherlands reminiscent of Goya's early paintings?" Pook inquires. "Was that before or after Godzilla ate Tokyo?" I ask. "The director's avant-garde use of the Coke bottle was intense," Pook tries. "Ya, made me very, very thirsty," I interject.

You can learn a lot about your lover by watching movies together. I have learned that Pootie only likes the super jumbo bucket of popcorn drenched in 40W motor oil when it costs five dollars and up. She will not let me drop my M & M's in the box to warm them up. If I should take more than two handfuls of popcorn, she grunts and shifts the box to the other side. This makes me suck and sulk on my cold M & M's. We always get the monster vessel of diet pop. For Pootie, this negates all of the calories from the popcorn and candy. Pootie always takes forty or fifty movie napkins, and makes a napkin quilt for her lap. Is she afraid to get the seat or floor dirty?

Sometimes we meet our friends at the movies. No sooner than we are seated, and sometimes even before we get our coats off, the assembly line of munchies starts moving. This lets everyone participate in tasting and shifting. We all noticed at the second go-around that the popcorn was missing. Pootie thought that we wouldn't notice, but you gotta have something salty in between gum drops and chocolate lumps. It taps your fillings back into place. We had to chip in for a second tub of popcorn because Pootie wouldn't share. Our friends and I have learned to accept this, because we know that one tub of popcorn will keep Pootie happy for hours on end. This is a fine group of women who will toss in two whole boxes of M. & M's and let them get nice and mushy.

We never, never, never leave a movie before it's over, no matter how bad it is, or how much I sigh in disgust. We have got to get the last thirty-five-cent's worth of pain in. Pootie will let me go and have a smoke, only if I have the car keys; otherwise, I am captive to the bitter end. She will, on occasion, give me the empty bucket so that I am kept busy breaking my molars on the burnt popcorn seeds.

Pootie and I have seen over three hundred movies together. We like the lesbian movies the best. It is the only time we run into every other lesbian we have ever known and get a chance to catch up on old times.

People ask us why we still go to the movies when VCR's and tape rentals are cheaper. I think that the big screen offers more excitement. A closeup view of a quivering nostril hair often adds depth to the plot. Nonetheless, I have a bone to pick with movie plots. They need help.

TODAY'S MOVIE PLOTS

♂♀ *BOY GETS GIRL.*

♂♀ *MIDDLE AGED MAN GETS YOUNG GIRL.*

♂♀ *OLD MAN GETS YOUNG GIRL WHO IS CRAZY ABOUT HIM.*

♂♀♀ *MECHANICALLY ENHANCED MAN GETS TWO GIRLS AND MAJOR TUNE UP.*

♂♀ *MAN GETS GIRL, SURROUNDED BY EVIL GAY PEOPLE.*

TODAY'S GAY MOVIE PLOTS

♂♂ *MAN MEETS MAN, GETS DISEASES AND DIES.*

♀♀♀ *WOMAN MEETS TWO WOMEN AND GOES CELIBATE.*

♀♀ *WOMAN MEETS WOMAN AND THEY KILL THEMSELVES.*

♀♂♀ *WOMAN LOVES WOMAN, BUT THE WHITE KNIGHT (MALE, OF COURSE) IN SHINING ARMOR DELIVERS HER FROM A LIFE OF SIN.*

PLOTS I'D LIKE TO SEE

☺ *WOMAN MEETS WOMAN, HAS A LONG LOVING RELATIONSHIP AND LIVES HAPPILY EVER AFTER.*

☺ *WOMAN MEETS MANY WOMEN AND HAS A WONDERFUL SUCCESSFUL LIFE EXPLORING ALL OF THE POSSIBILITIES.*

☺ *MAN MEETS MAN OR WOMAN MEETS WOMAN AND TOGETHER THEY SAVE THE WORLD FROM EVIL STRAIGHT PEOPLE.*

Yo, Jody Foster, are ya listening?

Sundering Friendships

Couples you know and love will break up from time to time. When this happens, you and your lover may be forced to choose sides and/or friendships. Should you like them both equally, at best you will be put into the unenviable position of traitor by one of them. Following are a few guidelines that have never worked for us.

Pootie and I throw two parties a year. We are not the party animals we once were. We'd like to have more parties, but the trauma of assembling a guest list leaves us cold. Before you throw a party, know who is going with whom. Make a list of all of your friends and cross reference from time to time. Nothing kills a party atmosphere quicker than a recently broken pair, screaming and hissing at each other from across the room.

If a couple you know has broken up, try to find out who is the dumper and who is the dumpee. This is very important. You will want to invite the dumper over first. She is happy: she is looking, or she is with someone else. She is usually over the relationship faster.

You may not like your friend's new chosen partner. You must know the new woman's name. Never call her by the ex's first name. This is why words like "darling" were invented. In a pinch, name tags can be life savers. Often one of your friends will choose a new mate that has a body to die for, but the intellectual capacity of clam dip. Be polite and introduce her to all of the other women there.

Always give the dumpee some time to get over her heartbreak; otherwise, she will spend all evening crying over the guacamole, pestering everyone with "Remember when" stories.

Should you decide to maintain both friendships with a sundering couple, you will have to deceive them both. I once made the mistake of telling a friend that I was going to have lunch with her recent ex. Not only did I have a rotten lunch, I was thoroughly interrogated twice. Funny, they both asked the same questions. "How did she look?" "What was she wearing?" "What did she say? About me?" "Who is she seeing now?" "You've got to be kidding!" "How do you think she really feels?" Answer in the oblique. "She looks fine." Do not say, "She looks great; she has lost ten pounds and she's radiant." "She was wearing some green thing" is safer than "She had the most fabulous sweater I've ever seen." "We didn't talk that much" is better than "She dazzled me with stories of all her new adventures." "I don't know who she is seeing now" is safe.

Never, never, never discuss or describe the new love interest to the ex. You have seen nothing, and you know nothing. Otherwise, you will be forced to answer questions like "Is she older than I?" "Is she thinner than I?" "Are her eyes bluer than mine?" Let the ex-lover discover all about the new love interest from someone else.

Never take sides when a couple you know is breaking up. Smile, be sympathetic, but keep your opinions to yourself. If the original couple reunites, they will only remember what you said about them.

It has been our experience that it will take over a year before it is safe to have the original couple meet face to face in a party setting. A good sign is when they are both seeing someone else.

Should you and your mate be hermit lesbians, it is good to know that through sundering relationships, your circle of friends and contacts will continue to expand and grow.

Lugging Life's Possessions

This morning on our bed, there are twenty neat little piles of clothing. With just a glancing inventory, I see five pair of slacks, fourteen shirts, twenty undies and ten pair of socks. You would think that we were packing for an extended stay in Tibet. No, Pootie is packing for a weekend in Chicago. Pootie is busy dragging out the big suitcase from the attic, the one that could easily carry two dead bodies. This is so she has somewhere to put me after I drop dead from exhaustion hauling her trousseau.

I point out my neatly packed weekender with pride. Pootie, unimpressed, asks if I have extra room in it for the two umbrellas she's taking, just in case. Having once been a Girl Scout, she firmly believes in the motto of always being prepared. I have two ruptured discs to attest to her beliefs.

Most of our relationship has been one of love, togetherness, and the schlepping of heavy objects about the planet. No matter where we are, one of us is lugging a bag, box, or piece of luggage. All of our vacation photos show us with a bug-eyed, strained, sweaty look.

Bell hops across the country have stood agape after opening the side door of our car, assuming that we are part of a gypsy caravan. It always costs us twenty dollars to have our luggage brought up to a room. It's not that we are big tippers, we feel obligated to contribute to the cost of his new truss.

Pootie watches all those National Geographic Specials on how Nomadic tribes move their entire village on camels. She will take notes on how to fold a tent to resemble a napkin for future reference.

I have finally figured out why Pootie is so well prepared. It seems she takes great pride in announcing "We have it!" should I request something while on vacation. This is very comforting only when you are in Alaska, and toothpaste is fourteen dollars a tube.

Last month we decided to visit our local zoo for the afternoon. Pootie took a small suitcase that looked like a diaper bag covered in tapestry. By her grunt as she threw it into the back seat, I guesstimated that it weighed fifteen pounds. While waiting for her to find a pair of mukluks (just in case it snowed), I glanced through the bag to see what she couldn't live without. Inside were three oranges, two cans of pop, a wash cloth and a small towel, napkins, sunscreen, lip balm, change, a tire pressure gauge, hand cream, corn pads, extra cigarettes, tissue, sun visors, Band-aids, and an extra pair of socks. If we had an emergency of any type, we were ready.

I don't remember much about the exotic wildlife we saw that day. I wonder if the animals remember a panting red-faced woman leaning on their cages for a rest.

Creepy Critters

Every woman in the universe is afraid of something. The odds of your both being afraid of the exact same thing will be rare. It would be very nice if the both of you took on the responsibility of capturing all the creepy critters that you'll encounter in your lifetime. Unfortunately, this task was bestowed upon me.

I remember the day I was drafted, only because Pootie was standing on our commode, flailing her arms and screaming at the top of her lungs. The way she was carrying on, I thought that a forty-foot python had slithered into the tub. I was wrong. It was an itsy-bitsy spider. With a wisp of toilet paper and a few high jumps, I managed to slay the minuscule monster. Pootie, overjoyed, threw her arms around me and thanked me over a hundred times. You tend to remember the riveting times in a relationship. I was thus assigned the job of creepy critter removal.

I can easily handle the occasional spider; however, the critters I've been removing lately have been getting bigger. There have been flies, wasps, bee hives, a random mouse, and the two full grown cats PuPu accidentally ran over with the car. Large dead road kill is also on the agenda now. I have had to remove one flat racoon and a decomposing mole from the front of our house. I tried to reason with Pootie that since she did not kill these creatures, I should not be responsible for their removal.

Pootie then did her big trick of fake swooning. She only resorts to this in cases of emergency. She rests her arm over her eyes, and sighs the sigh of "If you don't fix this, I'm going to die!" Fake swooning is the only thing that will make me go and get the bag and gloves and clothes pin for my nose, and remove the offending object without question.

Pootie insists that all of the creepy critters have a proper burial. Our yard is starting to look a lot like a cemetery. Throwing them in the trash in considered a sacrilege, unless it is the dead of winter and the ground is frozen solid. Even then, I have stood more than once with my hand over my heart, reverently praying over a trash can in sub-zero temperatures.

Comforting Pootie after these episodes is trying. I never really know what to say. "No, PuPu, it's not your fault. You didn't know the cat was asleep under your back tires" sounds good, but "I am sure the spider is much happier in spider heaven" doesn't sound all that sincere.

Last summer, Pootie made me remove the fly paper because she doesn't want the insects to languish. I must smote with haste to keep her swooning to a minimum. This has led to frenzied killing in the middle of the night when she hears any buzzing and I want some sleep. Naming the deceased has become rather burdensome. We're up to Ms. Fly No. 2005.

It is now late fall, and I have dug a few extra plots in the yard this year. I saw a very decrepit squirrel yesterday. And even though we have put paper owls in every patio window, at least one pigeon will kamikaze itself into birdie heaven before Christmas. Pootie mentioned something about boxing the critters instead of using a plastic bag. I refused to make mini coffins, although two popsicle sticks glued together do make a wonderful cross.

Much joy and sadness has filled our hearts with the handicapped critters that we have tried to save over the years. Caruso comes immediately to mind.

She was an infant starling that fell out of the nest. Only two ounces and completely featherless, but chirping. She lost the use of her feet for perching, so I made her a sling. Her voice was strong and loud. I, being an idiot, thought that she would need worms to eat. After searching for hours and recreating the Grand Canyon in our yard, I found a big fat night crawler. I didn't have the heart to chop up the worm, and Pootie refused to let me use the Cuisine-art or the blender. After a few hurried calls, we found out that canned puppy food would be just as good. Greatly relieved, we fed and watered, and sang to Caruso every four hours, around the clock. She was eating and chirping and pooping with gusto. In the three weeks we nursed her, we were able to experience the miracle of feather formation. We exercised her little birdie legs everyday, hoping to get her to perch. We rocked her gently to strengthen her wings. Caruso passed away twenty-two days after she entered our lives. We have learned that even the smallest of creatures is always a wonder to behold.

Time Warps

"I'm ready!" Pook calls out. I get up, get another can of pop, look over the TV Guide and change channels. I do not move toward the door until Pootie is standing next to it with her coat on. I have learned that to Pootie, getting ready to go anywhere is a long involved experience. "I'm ready!" Pook chants. I light a fresh cigarette and think about washing the car.

Every woman on this planet comes with her own inner timetable. I have always been on a rather expeditious schedule. I always arrive early. I was a preemie. If I am supposed to be somewhere at, say, ten o'clock, you can bet your bottom dollar I'm there at nine forty-five and pacing. PuPu's timetable is set according to the millennia. She thinks in terms of epochs, while I count off milliseconds.

You will never be able to change someone's inner timetable. I sincerely hope that this little piece of advice will save you two, maybe three, aneurysms during your relationship.

The first proclamation of "I'm ready!" means that Pook's decided that she wants to go somewhere. I lie back on the sofa or build an addition to the house. The second declaration of "I'm ready!" means Pook has chosen what to wear. I make coffee and re-tile the bathroom. The third pronouncement of "I'm ready!" means she has brushed her hair and found the car keys. It's usually the fifth "I'm ready!" that gets me up and moving.

Unaware of inner timetable conflicts when we first moved in together, I would stupidly pop right up and put on my coat. All I got out of this was five pounds slimmer from basting, and mad as hell at having to wait. Pook could not understand why I was red-faced and screaming at her every time she got into the car. We had to adjust to each other's inner timetable. We accomplished this by my nagging and Pook's taking her sweet time. Our conversations go like this: "We have to be there in an hour!" I remind her sweetly. I put on my coat, and take the car for a wash and fill-up, and do any nearby errands. Upon my return, I continue to nag, counting off the minutes like a loud atomic clock, "We have six minutes to get there." This conversation always ends with "#%*&%%!!! We're a half hour late!" PuPu and I have had this interplay each day for over ten years. To Pootie's credit, she can make a deadline if she has to, although I have yet to experience a movie without running to our seats.

Timetables conflicts are interesting when experiencing art galleries. I like to walk briskly through a museum, glancing at art while keeping my pulse up. Pootie is often still admiring the entrance archway as I exit the building. We now arrange to meet sometime later, so that I am not breathing down the back of her neck and my public nagging is kept to a minimum. I sometimes satellite around her, telling her what's to come, or what's on sale at the museum's gift shop while she is contemplating O'Keefe's use of red. This seems to work for us.

All in all, we've adjusted pretty well. We now fully understand that she is the sloth and I am the humming bird in life's adventures. I pace, pull my hair out and nag, and Pootie turns up the stereo so she can't hear me.

Haunting Sexual Ms.Adventures

Poke and I do the same things in bed that all red blooded lesbians do; but after five years and three thousand wonderful encounters, we decided to add some variety to our sex life. We purchased a few erotic books with titles like **Mary, Debbie and Sue in Bondage**. You know, the cheap books we've all purchased at sometime for $1.98. No plot, just "Hello," raw sex and "Goodbye." The same books that no one admits to owning. Don't you wonder why it is a ten-million dollar industry when no one buys them? We also went to the local discount house and purchased two hundred yards of clothes line. Our bondage episode died a very quick death. Poke was a Girl Scout for many years, and the sight of all that rope made her want to show me the four hundred knots that she thought she remembered. After her fiftieth try at the double ended loop knot that is used to secure grisly bears at campsite, I fell asleep. The dirty books were scanned once and tossed under the bed along with the rope and forgotten.

All these things were unceremoniously presented to us on moving day, by a six-foot, two-hundred pound male. He had the damnedest smirk on his face as he announced: "Ladies, you forgot to pack these; I found them under the bed." Mortified, we avoided the movers for the rest of the day.

If you clean your house like I do, remember to look under all the beds BEFORE YOU MOVE.

Survival Skills

"Oh shit!" Pook mumbles under her breath. "We were supposed to get off at that exit!" The sign looming up in front of me says "Next Exit in forty-two miles." I bite my tongue and say nothing--she's doing the best that she can.

When Pook and I travel by car, she reads the map and gives directions while I drive. This arrangement evolved when Pook discovered that I could not identify one State from another on a map. I will fearlessly drive anywhere if I am told how to get there. Pook is wonderful at giving directions and will even count aloud the number of remaining streets to a turn, on occasion. On the Interstate highways, this gets a tad more difficult when the traffic signs are misleading; so every once in a while, we get to see the exciting perimeter of a State. This has made me change my driving habits. I have been known to do heart palpitating ninety-degree turns across five lanes of traffic at fifty-five miles per hour and up. Pook's lips purse and I can feel an "Oh shit!" coming out; I know: this is the exit we are supposed to be on. With only five feet of exit ramp available, I look heavenly toward the goddess and swerve. No accidents so far, but I know we have doubled the income of cardiac surgeons across America.

Pook and I travel a lot by car. We're cheap, and I'm afraid to fly, so we drive everywhere. Last month, we drove to Texas. This was a relatively easy trip, consisting of three twelve-hour days of driving. We left Michigan in the middle of a blizzard, so we had to ice-skate through Ohio. Being from the motor capital of the world, driving twelve hundred miles is considered a jot down the road.

Funny, some of the odd things we take with us on a long drive. I always take a vehicular bag of fruit, so that we will have something nutritional to snack on in between McIngots. We never really eat this fruit. We just move it around the vehicle. Depending on the season, all the fruit ripens within two or three hours. We never throw it away until we get home. Our Texas trip lasted ten days, and that last bag of festering fruit kicked open the trunk lid somewhere in Omaha and jumped to a merciful death by itself.

Pook drives when she absolutely has to, and when it is really life saving. Pook drove us up Pike's Peak. I should have known that Pike's Peak was going to be interesting when at the entrance, a State Trooper was feeling the tires of an exiting car. Inquiring lesbians want to know. He mumbled something about brake failure. Stupidly, we paid our nine bucks and continued on. The first couple of corkscrew turns were panoramic and serene. As we continued our ascent minus any security railing and passed the first eagle, I got uneasy. I started to panic when we passed our first cloud. Around the time that the surrounding city looked like a fly spec on the earth's surface, I slid to the car floor clutching a rosary to my bosom, and began screaming about my life being over. Bravely Pook continued to drive. With nothing but the sky and sheer mountain wall to guide her, Pook pushed gallantly upward. Good thing she drove. If it had been me, I'd still be up there, clutching the ground. The descent was just as frightening, only we knew it would be over soon. Much sooner, if the brakes failed.

Traveling by car can be a wonderful experience. We have learned a lot about ourselves this way. Did you know that the statement, "I think we're in Nebraska" is not one bit frightening if you have been driving for eighteen consecutive hours and are going in that general direction anyway? At sixty five miles per hour, you can easily eat a three-course dinner, enjoy a milk shake, and drive without a mishap. Rest assured that the one thing you packed in the back of the trunk will be the very thing you will need on a non-stop turnpike. The only two things played on radio stations outside of any metropolis are Elton John records and country western music. There is a McDonald's every six hundred feet, so you will gain three pounds for every two hundred miles that you travel by car. Duet whistling will make both of you have fits of laughter for three hundred miles, and keep passing weirdos away. A hot shower and a warm bed can be much better than sex.

There is a world of difference between city miles and vacation miles. With city miles, your corner store is at the corner. Vacation miles are something else altogether. The corner store is fifty miles down the road, and the cute restaurant where you go to dinner is seventy three miles from your campsite.

You will recognize vacation miles by the vague terms that people use to describe distance. "UP THE ROAD A PIECE" could be referring to the next town or galaxy. "We're almost there." Sit back and have a snack; you are at least twenty minutes away from your destination. "Just over yonder." This place is never found. Like the Bermuda Triangle, no one has ever gotten here. This term is used to drive tourists mad.

Home Remedies

Pook is stirring her caldron, and the fumes emanating are loosening the kitchen wallpaper. It's just about ready now. I sit shivering in the corner, not so much from the cold I have, but from the anticipation of what's to come. Pook is whipping up a batch of her home remedy for colds. It contains chicken fat, horseradish, one rutabaga, and a dollop of mustard for color. She renders these ingredients into a paste that is spread onto a piece of cheesecloth. This searing odorous covering is then slammed against my chest before it disintegrates. I am then bound tightly with plastic wrap. In a pinch, a fifty-gallon trash bag is cut to size. Pook tells me that this is done to keep the vapors in. I see the spoon starting to dissolve as she stirs. It's ready now. Involuntarily, I cough. There is no escape. I am to be a victim of love torture again.

There is a frightening glint in my Pootie's eyes as she prepares her remedy. Disgusting things are found in pouches, and with a shovel in the middle of the night. About the only thing she doesn't do are incantations. She knows that would really freak me out. "I haven't killed anybody yet!" Pook boasts. Shall I be the first? Are any of your ex's missing? "It doesn't taste half as bad as it smells!" Does that mean that I will gag and writhe for only five minutes, as opposed to ten? Neither of those statements are particularly reassuring.

My only home remedy involves a fifth of whiskey and honey added for taste. This particular remedy doesn't actually cure your cold, but after just a few doses, you don't care if you have one. For some strange reason, I firmly believe that aloe vera gel can cure every skin problem, including leprosy. I have never applied aloe vera to a leprous rash, but I feel quite confident with its magical properties. Oatmeal is oatmeal, except that colloidal oatmeal costs a fortune. Being a non-medical person, colloidal oatmeal sounded as if it was brimming with curing ingredients. Stupid me. Colloidal means very finely ground. This is very important if you get poison ivy as often as I do. Throw some regular uncooked oatmeal into a grinder. This will save you the price of this book in only two applications. Colloidal oatmeal, when added to your bath, is supposed to sooth a variety of rashes. I have never found this to be true; however, I know that you will want to try anything and everything to get relief.

Home remedies can be passed down from mother to daughter, through generations, or discovered and adapted to a particular ailment. Home remedies started out as solutions to cure the ills of ancient times. What scares me is that somewhere along the way, when eye of newt became scarce, vapor rub was substituted. I dare not ask Pook about the original formula for her plaster.

Every woman on this planet has her secret stash of home remedies. These remedies vary from pills and potions to elixirs. Home remedies have many things in common. They smell and taste bad, and have nothing to do with real medicine. Home remedies appear at the first sign of any illness. If you are not familiar with your lover's remedies, you will be subject to at least one application.

You can always tell when your partner is about to delve into the realm of home remedies. You will see things in the kitchen that do not belong together. Their medicinal hoard will be laid out and inspected.

There may be whispered phone calls to relatives using words like "pinch," "plug," "tincture," and "smidgen." You will be ill, and all of the drug stores will be closed. Big pots are brought forth. Rubber gloves, goggles and a face mask may appear. You might catch a glimpse of an ancient book, or yellow stained papers. This will be the only time in your life that you willingly want to go to your mother's, unless her remedies are worse.

No matter how you stock up on good sound medicines, your Pootie will try a home remedy every so often. This is to maintain her conjuring skills should the local apothecary go defunct. After all, they have only been operating for ninety-six years. You can bet your bottom dollar, she has obscure medicinal shards older than that.

Pook can cure just about anything with her remedies. That's because you get better, or she'll whip up something new. Spontaneous recovery becomes a necessity with home remedies. Miracles can happen.

Slumbering

Sleeping together is much more than just sex. Believe it or not, when sleeping together, sex is the easiest part. It's the sleeping that may cause some problems. People have to adjust to sleeping together. Pook and I have very different sleeping habits. For me, sleeping is a passive activity, usually accomplished in the dark, with complete silence. Pootie likes to sleep with the radio playing softly in the background, and with enough night lights in place to make the bedroom resemble a night baseball game being played at Yankee Stadium. Her cat Smokey jumps on and off the bed fifty or sixty times a night, just to announce his presence. All of this activity required major adjustments on my part.

Unexplainable things happen at night. The radio station always plays super weird music in the middle of the night; so upon awakening you often wonder if you are still on your mother planet. It will take some time, but you can get used to a glaring cat eyeball or intimate cat parts at microscopic range when opening your eyes. The gravitational pull of the planet changes at night. Your sweetie's little leg, draped lovingly over yours, will weigh in the G-force factors after only ten minutes. Beware of the deadly pointed elbow. It will search and destroy the softest part of your body. Stereo snoring (hers and the cat's) will eventually drive you mad, or lull you into a comatose state.

It will be beneficial to find a mate that has the same temperature range as you do. On the thermometer scale of life, Pook is a lizard and I am a penguin. Pook is into thermal nuclear sleep. Every night she uses an electric blanket, a heating pad for her neck, and a bed warmer. All of these devices are set at four thousand degrees Fahrenheit or so. This is akin to informing your body that it is now a baked potato roasting every night. Pook asks me why I don't like to cuddle up with her like I used to. I think it's because it is very difficult to snuggle up to a blast furnace. If one of us ever has a hot flash, we'll come very close to a total meltdown. When you combine all of these factors, you begin to see how sleeping together takes on the momentum of an Olympic event.

This is the same woman who doesn't want to cuddle in the summertime because it is too hot. To me, the conditions are identical. Sweltering, humid, and sweaty. Pook tells me that this is a different kind of heat. She was very surprised when I had that fourteen-ton air-conditioner installed last summer. When this machine is turned all the way up to arctic, we are able to indulge in snow storms in mid-July. The snow angels we make on the carpet turn into very nice cuddling experiences. I highly recommend it. Mukluks and ear muffs make very interesting bedroom attire.

Clothes Ponies

Clothing for women is much more than just a covering for the body. Clothes often represent a woman's mood and individuality. Pootie and I try to express a lifestyle through our garment choices. Unfortunately, we often look like we are attending two different functions at the same time. Today is a perfect example. Pootie looks like she is off to a fox hunt. I look like I'm on my way to a luau. In reality, we're on our way to lunch at Taco City.

I like to commit fashion genocide when I dress. I am making a statement with what I wear, but you have to speak fluent Greek to understand what I am saying. I like vivid colors. The more the better. I often wear a plethora of neon pink, and electric blue, with dashes of fuscia. Bright colors cheer me up.

Comfort is the next garment essential for me. Caftans, mumus, and sweats were the best apparel ever invented. What else can you cover the broadside of a barn in comfortably? I wasn't always this way. I used to wear high heels, a girdle, and panty hose. Somewhere around age of forty I stopped trying to containerize myself. I have been in expando heaven ever since. Spandex means to me what cashmere means to others. It washes and wears well. It is impervious to stains, and will expand to meet the unexpected needs of a ninety-nine-cent pancake breakfast.

Unhesitatingly, I will combine clothing themes to suit my needs. I will wear a mumu, running shoes and a fanny pack if I am spending the day shopping interrupted only by an all-you-can-eat brunch. Every year or so, I have a fling with fluff. I will buy a caftan with lace, or a jogging suit with stripes to infer Olympian couch potato status. PuPu never says anything derogatory about an outfit I have chosen. She can flatter me into changing by simply saying, "Great outfit! It adds ten years and twenty pounds to you!" I will rip the ensemble from my body immediately as if it were radioactive and never don it again.

Pootie and I often order our clothes through catalogs. This is making UPS very rich. I mistakenly presume that an outfit will look as good in a size eighteen as it does on the size-four model displaying it.

PuPu favors clothes that look wonderful if she were going on a safari, fly-fishing, or playing polo. I lovingly refer to Pook's ensembles as gorilla wear. Thigh-high wading boots and a hunting vest look a tad pompous at our local mall, although a grouse pocket comes in quite handy during a super sale. Practicality does not enter into Pootie's clothing choices. She has English hunting shirts that are dry clean only. I have a hard time believing the first thing the gentry did after a good day of hunting was to zip over to the dry cleaners. Most of her other stuff has to be ironed. I am the only one willing to flatten garments without burning holes into them. This is where bartering and finagling comes into our relationship. I refuse to iron anything that is going to be smashed into her closet.

Over the years, Pootie has commandeered all of the closet space, and zealot stockpiling has resulted in overflowing closets. We are only able to close the closet doors by throwing our combined weight against them until we hear the hinges click. Bruised shoulders have caused me to take action. Once a year, when Pootie is in a good mood, spring is in the air, and all of the planets are in alignment, I will announce, "It's time to clean out your closet!" This used to greatly alarm Pootie, until she figured out a way to thwart me. She simply wears me down with an all-day fashion show, complete with detailed explanations of why each outfit is still good. Now that sixties fashions are returning, I also hear two hundred resounding choruses of "It's back in style!" So that I do not feel totally vanquished, Pook will discard one old belt that she will donate to a local charity. Technically, she never throws anything away.

Motif footwear is Pook's priority this year. She owns a pair of combat boots that will never see any military duty; a gorgeous pair of riding boots that will never feel a blade of grass, let alone a horse's hide, because she doesn't want to get them dirty; and a pair of tennis shoes with soles that have engineered rocking chambers. Their price suggests that they should catapult you at least once to the moon free.

Yes, you can learn a lot from your mate's clothing choices. I have learned how to make slipcovers and trampolines out of my old mumus, and to always wear shoulder pads before I take a running start to close the closet doors.

Bathroom Or Bust

I believe there should be a constitutional amendment stating that "For every two women residing together, there shall be a minimum of two, preferably three, bathrooms." This doctrine should be an inalienable right for all lesbian couples residing in one dwelling, because no two women feel the same way about a bathroom, Pook and I included. Sharing one bathroom has put a strain on our relationship.

We have one and a half baths at our house. The half bath is alcoved in the dungeon of our basement, which is cold, and damp, and the local V.F.W. for all the bugs in town. We only use it when we have to.

For me, a bathroom is a personal maintenance room that one visits on occasion, and doesn't stay very long. Pootie feels that the bathroom is the life source of the universe, and will remain entombed in there for hours on end. (Not surprisingly, she will also list comforting as an adjective for porcelain). This leaves me with no alternative but to visit the dungeon, where I can watch a variety of bugs trying to attack my legs. Every evening Pootie will announce, "I am going to the bathroom!" She will then disappear for three days. If she is silent for more than two hours, I will tap at the door and inquire if she has died on the pot. "No, I'm just contemplating life!" she merrily retorts. Exasperated, I grab the fly swatter and go to the dungeon.

I feel that a shower should last six minutes, tops. You soap, shampoo, rinse, and you're out. Pootie believes that our sixty-gallon water heater was installed for her personal use, and that it should be drained completely before her shower is over. Unfortunately, the billowing steam is loosening the tiles in the foyer three rooms away, and our water bills resemble our mortgage payments. I have to get up an hour earlier and beat her to the bathroom to enjoy any resemblance of hot water. Otherwise, I have to wait two hours till the tank refills and reheats.

We disagree on what should be hung in a bathroom. I want only towels and a wash cloth. Pootie likes to hang a week's worth of what she calls rinsables, which are either floating in the sink or dangled over every knob and rack in the room. As far as I can determine, rinsables are really washables that

Pook is unable to let out of her sight. Our bathroom has a moist, Victoria's-Secret-jungle aura about it. Today's exhibit includes panty hose, shoe laces, one bra, three knee highs, and an untouchable, unmentionable soaking in the sink.

After I swath myself into the shower, I must stand very still. There are thirty bottles balanced precariously around the tub and in every nook and cranny. One false move and there could be an avalanche of particulars that should never be mixed. I use only the products that I can recognize, after once shampooing my head with a deodorant crystal and pumicing my teeth. I must admit that for two consecutive weeks, my hair smelled great and my teeth were never whiter.

Should you ever come over for a visit, we have a smorgasbord of soap on display. You have your choice of big slimy mushy bars, or minuscule rose soapettes, which I will gladly pay twenty bucks to anyone able to make the damn things froth. There are six consecrated guest towels that I am never allowed to use because I live here. Our toilet bowl water comes in a rainbow of color with a mountain fresh scent. On the two occasions that I have ridden our porcelain bus, the mountain fresh scent was not all that memorable. The coup de grace is the fish sculpture Pootie put on the lid of the toilet tank. She says it adds ambience. That must be when it stabs you in the back every time you sit down.

If I should win the lottery, sell five million books, or ever have four thousand dollars burning a hold in my pocket, the first thing I'm going to get is a brand new bathroom. Paraphernalia-free, Pootie-free, and bug-free. Till then, I'll have to settle for a large can of RAID and a new fly swatter.

Threats vs. Nagging

A Threat, by definition, is a verbal utterance of varying lengths articulated to another for the purpose of making said other fall to the ground and beg for mercy. The exposure of a secret fear of another. Malice aforethought. Psychological murdering, torture, or T.K.O. of a human being with words.

Examples: *"That's it! I've had enough! We're through!" "I'm gonna tell your mother!" "I'm gonna tell your boss!" or "I'm gonna tell Oprah Winfrey!"*

To be really effective, a threat must be used very sparingly. A severe tone of voice adds to the weight of a good threat. I personally have never seen my intended victim fall prostrate and beg for mercy. A flash of fury is the most I've ever seen. If the threat is repeated too often, the victim will no longer exhibit any symptoms whatsoever. There is nothing worse than a good threat cast off with a "So what!" or the deadly "Go ahead!" Threats are really modern day ego smacking with a gauntlet. Since it is fairly hard to get a decent gauntlet these days, threats are a cheap and effective replacement. Unfortunately, threats are supposed to lead to an action. Not everyone wants to take action to back up her threats, so we invented nagging instead.

Nagging is repeated verbal indoctrination. Nagging is often used as an oral reminder to do or not to do something. Let's face it, nagging is a threat that is sugar-coated and repeated ad nauseam. Also known as Tautology. Nagging, if done correctly, can drive the other person crazy.

Example:

Let's say you are supposed to take out the trash on Monday morning. A professional nagger will start on Monday night the week before with: Did you remember to take the trash out?" or "Did they pick up our trash today?"

Tuesday: "We have to remember to take out the trash."

Wednesday: "Boy, we sure do have a lot of trash."

Thursday: "Do we have enough garbage cans to fit all of the trash in?"

Friday: "They are having a sale on trash cans at K-Mart."

Sunday night: "You won't forget to take out the trash, will you, Sweetie?"

Your only recourse to nagging is a threat. "If you mention the trash ONE MORE TIME, I'm going to drag it into the house and pile it up in the living room!" Pook knows that I would never do this, so I am reduced to using the invaluable device known as the ACCUSATION!

My favorite accusation is "How could you?" This is a wonderful accusation as far as accusations go, because it is ambiguous while insinuating guilt. This technique foists the responsibility back to the tautologer and completely changes the subject. A strongly uttered "HOW COULD YOU!!!" will save you from having to make good on your threat; unfortunately, it won't stop the nagging.

Home Improvements

Things are going to break where you live. Even if you are structurally blessed beyond your wildest dreams, your partner will want at the very least to add shelving somewhere in your abode. Home improvements can be time consuming, expensive, and migraine producing.

We ventured into the world of home improvements the day PuPu bought a new toilet seat on sale. We thought we knew how to put on a new toilet seat. It took us only two weeks and several hundred dollars to install it. First we oiled, wrenched, and cussed the old seat off. In this endeavor, we cracked the main porcelain fixture while it was full of water. A toilet holds a lot of water. We then had to rent a wet vac. Toilets weigh a lot, too. They are bolted to the floor, and are not easy to remove. By the way, there is a pipe connection that should be shut off to keep wet vacuuming to a minimum. Plumbers are expensive. They make most of their money on the weekend disasters we self-fix people do to save a few bucks. After giving the plumber enough money to get her children a good college education, we tried our hand at installing shelves.

We studied up on installing shelving first. We rented an instructional video and bought a top-of-the-line stud finder. We watched the video a hundred times. We aligned the stud finder at the corner and began. It would beep every four inches. We would bang a nail in the wall every four inches, never hitting a stud. Come to find out, there were old pipes in the back of that wall, which we were able to see quite clearly after the first two hundred holes. The shelves cost only forty dollars. The carpenter we had to hire to do it right cost us five hundred. She said she had never seen so-o-o many holes in one wall before. It took three days to replaster.

We have a saying here, "Anything worth doing is worth doing four or five times." This is because we have yet to get any improvement right on the first try. Shop was not offered to me in high school back when dinosaurs roamed the Earth, and Pootie never picked up a hammer or built anything in her forty odd years. Undaunted, we thought we had several things going for us. We were naive, enthusiastic, and hopeful.

May I mention that none of these attributes had helped us with any improvement so far.

Our final improvement cost us four thousand dollars. We tried to re-tar the driveway. It would have been much cheaper if I had remembered to post a sign that read "HOT TAR--DO NOT ENTER." Who could have known that all four tires on the mail truck would melt so-o-o quickly? There was the additional cost of two hair cuts to remove the tar from our heads. We had to burn all of our clothes, shoes and gloves, because they were tar-soaked, too. We also purchased a gallon of petroleum jelly to get all the tar off our skin, and three thousand dollars to the licensed asphalt company that did it right.

Now when a screw falls off anything in the house, we immediately call a professional. We have found that it saves us much money, time, and aggravation in the long run.

Holiday Hell

It's the week in between Christmas and New Year's. Pook and I are sitting in the den with one lit candle, and music playing ever so softly in the background. Sounds like the scenario for a wonderful romantic evening, except for the time of the year. For approximately ten days every year, we live like bandits hiding out from the F.B.I., only it's the holiday season and we're hiding out from our relatives.

I get up and bang my shin on the coffee table while going to check the answering machine. One of our relatives has been calling incessantly. Uttering a few cuss words, I braille myself back to the den. Pook whispers for me to bring the flashlight, so she can find her way to the bathroom without encountering anything painful in her path. Not much longer now, just four more days and nights to go. I peer cautiously through the blinds. No one's in the driveway. "All clear to flush!" I call to Pook.

Pook and I dreaded any holiday season because it meant that we had to endure families and assorted relatives for endless boring hours. Don't get me wrong, our relatives are no worse than most. There's weird aunt Agnes, with whom I have had the identical conversation for twenty years. "How you doing, auntie Agnes?" "Fine, just fine, Susan. Would you get me a beer?" "My name is Stacy," I remind her. Aunt Agnes is in her nineties. Breathing and drinking beer are her only activities. I have accepted the fact that I will always be a Susan to her. I have other assorted aunts that only ask why I'm not married yet and having babies. After thirty years they still cling to the belief that my lesbianism is a passing phase, and even though my menopause is on the horizon, they still fervently hope that I will proliferate. I also have a few uncles who stay mesmerized by any sports broadcast, with whom I have not communicated for decades, other than to ask who's winning.

Interaction in my family revolves around heated conversations about ailments, deaths, doctors, and prescribed medications. My family screeches and screams at each other. If you have a modulated voice, you will never be heard or believed. Shouting your words seems to add weight to your statement. Banging your fist on the table makes whatever you're saying gospel. Pook tells me that her family is exactly the same.

We did not always live in abeyance. This is the result of tradition tampering. Pootie and I were in our late thirties before we realized that we had suffered enough. In an effort to make our holidays more enjoyable, we tried to alter tradition. Our first change began with location. We invited both families to our house. This was a big mistake. Having thirty people over is a big expense. Having fifteen women in your kitchen, all trying to prepare one meal is a nightmare. Everyone wants to do it their way. We ended up with enough stuffing to fill the Grand Canyon, because no one would agree on the proper ingredients for a sacred holiday dressing. Good thing I remembered to put away the better dishes and accoutrements. I did not want my napkin rings used as ponytail holders or frisbees. We don't exactly roll out the holiday trough, but they are a homey bunch.

The mixing of the two clans was joyous for about two hours and one fifth of scotch. After that, they were fighting about everything from laxatives to global warming. Pook and I grabbed the egg nog and hid in the basement. We've been hiding out every holiday season since.

You can learn a lot of valuable information when you are stuck with your extended family. You will suddenly realize that you are the only sane person in the room. You may be struck by the thought that you have nothing in common with any of these people, and you would like not to visit with them ever again. You will feel chromosomally blessed, looking at your collective gene pool. Your mother may be the world's most wonderful person, but after six consecutive hours in her company, you will pray for an aneurism.

There are approximately twelve holidays per year, depending on your religious affiliation. Work-free, happy days given to us by the Goddess and the government. The good news is: A relationship gives you the opportunity to break free from Holiday Hell. This may cause some emotional upheaval with your family (they want you to suffer, too); surprise: they will survive.

Pook and I create our own traditions and holidays as we go along. We celebrate the day we first met, our first kiss, the first grey hair day, and any argument-free month. New Year's day is for sleeping in and getting over New Year's Eve. We even have a Goddess Day where we cater to each other's wishes.

Our retreat from Holiday Hell has been rather successful. Now, we get together with our respective families only every five years or so. Aunt Agnes has joined us in our holiday hiding. When she does see the family, she always sings the praises of her niece Susan, who lets her sit quietly in the basement for as long as she likes, with a glass and a whole keg of beer.

Till Death Do Us Part

Let's say that you and your beloved have been together for a few years. You love each other very much and you are acquiring things. Whether you are collecting furniture, records, or porcelain elephants, now is the time for you to make out your will. A will gives you peace of mind and protects your lover from all those vultures out there just waiting to pounce on your estate. REMEMBER, your lover has very few (if any) legal rights to your shared possessions. Please do not do this yourself, see a lawyer. This is no time to try and save a few bucks. You won't be here to inform the court of your intentions when they tell your lover that the five-dollar will kit is invalid due to some stupid error. Example: You signed the will on Sunday instead of Monday. Don't laugh, courts x-ray every document they come in contact with. Do you really want to test the system from the grave?

A will costs about three hundred dollars and is worth every cent. You don't have to tell your lover what you left or to whom, unless you want to. Pook and I did our wills through the same attorney, tucked them away in the safe deposit box and never discussed the details. Besides the distributing of my worldly possessions, I left specific instructions on how I would like my funeral conducted. If you have strong preferences about your funeral arrangements, I recommend that you include them in your will. Your attorney will be able to advise you as to whether your ashes can be scattered at thirty thousand feet. Your State may prohibit this.

Your lover may be in shock for some time after you are gone. So, instructions are very important. She is unlikely to remember what song you wanted played, and she could feel guilty for years that the wrong song was chosen. And, God forbid, she should go first. Her last wishes will become the most important things in your life. Contrary to popular belief, no one lives forever.

Your last will and testament is your last statement. To be really effective, this statement should piss all of your relatives off. It should give specific instructions on how to use your cash as padding in your coffin. It could describe in minute detail how the IRS should suck wind. It should leave your lawyer crying. Now is the time to be generous, bequeath everyone millions of dollars that you don't have.

Goddess Duty

Goddess Duty is the very fiber of a good relationship. It is all of the chores, jobs, and tasks that you perform only because you love your Pookie. Goddess Duties are the things that you would not do for another living soul on the face of the earth.

Goddess Duty is spending the afternoon with her Aunt Agnes, and patiently listening for the umpteenth time about how she walked to school barefoot and raised all twelve brothers and sisters single-handedly. It's when you walk her dog KILLER in the dead of winter, because you don't want your Pookie to catch cold. Going to committee meetings and smiling at the jerk next to you till your face hurts, because he's her boss. Goddess Duty includes the time you waited forever for a tow truck after sending her home in a cab. Laughing at the same joke she's been telling for the last two years. Buying her that coat she had her eye on but thought it was TOO expensive. Back rubs. Reading her horoscope first, every morning. Waxing her bicycle. Being her life-long cheerleader when she tries anything new and when she fails. Proudly displaying her art work and never wincing. Not nagging when she knows you're right. Listening to her new opera records without ear plugs. Not jumping for joy and shelling out fifty bucks for a head stone when KILLER goes to doggy heaven. Living with the horrible wallpaper just because she thought it was exquisite. Putting the coupons in her order, aisle by aisle, not the way you want them. Dabbing her with calamine lotion and not laughing when she gets poison ivy. Schlepping and cleaning the grill 'cause she feels like having a barbecue. Smiling and gnawing on what she has barbecued. Turning off the t.v., no matter what's on, because she wants to talk. Accepting the fact that the checkbook will never balance again. Consoling her and burying the cat she didn't see in the driveway. Taking a bite of her rutabaga fiber cookies. Holding her hand and telling her she's wonderful when she didn't get that promotion. Cutting the grass, waxing the floor, and cleaning the gutters because she hates it. Not going into a tirade every month when the bills come in. Patiently explaining for the twentieth time why the car has an "Oil" light. Doing the taxes 'cause she's just not good with figures.

Never saying anything negative about her family, even though they hate you with a passion. Buying a Barbie doll for all of your wool sweaters she accidentally shrank. Going where she wants to go on vacation, even though you've been there before.

If you are in a good relationship, I am sure that you can add hundreds of Goddess Duties that you have performed. Goddess Duties make a relationship last longer and her love for you stronger.

If your relationship is rocky or you are embarking on a new one, go ahead! Do your Duty! Be a Goddess today!

Interlacing

A wondrous thing begins to happen after the two of you have been together for a while. Your lives begin to "interlace," and the resulting pattern can be spectacular. Interlacing is a magical experience shared by two women who are developing a bonding union.

You will know that you and your Pootie are interlacing when you go to the market and she automatically pushes the cart while you read off the coupons. You are definitely interlacing when you go on a trip and you drive while she reads the map because you've always done it that way. Interlacing is also when you set the electric blanket at five because you know that's the way she likes it.

Interlacing is the time of a relationship when neither of you are on pins and needles. You both know what's expected of you. You have both relaxed in the warm feeling of love that surrounds you. You are starting to share and live each day as a pair.

Your Pootie has become more to you than a lover. She is now your soul mate, confidant, team mate, and partner. This is the wondrous part of your relationship where everything runs smoothly. Interlacing involves all the little rituals that you have invented for yourselves. It is during this time of a relationship that you begin to discover your strengths and weaknesses, your love, your devotion, and your faith in one another.

Around this same time, all of your friends will start thinking of you and your lover as a matched set. Like bookends, people are perceiving the two of you as a dyad. You are not losing your identify as an individual; rather, your personhood is expanding to embrace two. At every encounter with someone you know, you will be asked about your other.

It becomes quite amusing when your friends start to confuse the two of you, and they will. In our case, Pook is five feet four inches tall, has jet black hair, and weighs in at one hundred pounds. I am eight inches taller, have bright red hair, and weigh a lot closer than I'd like to two hundred pounds. You can see how we are easily mistaken for one another.

It is very nice to be perceived as part of a matched set. You belong to another, and feeling possessed in a non-demonic sense can be wonderful.

You'll have to excuse me for now. It's seven p.m. on Sunday night. Pootie will be turning on the television set. Without fail for the last sixteen years, we have watched "SIXTY MINUTES" together, and I always make the popcorn ♥

ORDER FORM

For additional copies of **Happily Ever After**, send check or money order for $10.00 per book (plus shipping and applicable sales tax) to:

SPECULATORS, INC.
P. O. BOX 99038
TROY, MICHIGAN 48099

Shipping: For each United States delivery address, add $2.00 for the first book, and $0.75 for each additional book. For each delivery address in Canada, add $2.50 for the first book, and $1.00 for each additional book. Overseas orders, add $5.00 for the first book, $2.50 for each addition book.

Sales Tax: Please add appropriate Sales Tax for books shipped to Michigan addresses.

Ship To (Please Print):

Name: _____

Address:_____

City: _____ State: _____ Zip: _____

Would you like the book(s) autographed?
_____ Yes _____ No